In full Bloem

Jamie Bloem – rugby footballer

Andrew Hardcastle

London League Publications Ltd

In full Bloem
Jamie Bloem – rugby footballer

© Andrew Hardcastle. Foreword © James Deighton

The moral right of Andrew Hardcastle to be identified as the author has been asserted.

Cover design © Stephen McCarthy.

Front cover: Jamie Bloem in action for Halifax (rlphotos.com)
Back cover: Referee! Jamie Bloem in charge of a match (rlphotos.com)

All photographs in this book are from private collections unless otherwise credited. No copyright has been intentionally breached; please contact London League Publications Ltd if you believe there has been a breach of copyright.

A CIP catalogue record for this book is available from the British Library.

First published in Great Britain in January 2013 by:
London League Publications Ltd, P.O. Box 65784, London NW2 9NS

ISBN:	978-1903659-65-6
Cover design by:	Stephen McCarthy Graphic Design 46, Clarence Road, London N15 5BB
Layout:	Peter Lush

Printed and bound in Great Britain by Charlesworth Press, Wakefield

Foreword

They say never judge a book by its cover and that adage couldn't be more accurate than when it is applied to Mr Jamie Justin Bloem.

It is a true honour to be asked to write a few words to introduce the man who over the last eight years or so has become one of my best friends. Initially I knew of Jamie by reputation only, his colourful and controversial playing career is documented in the following pages, though in many ways it does him an injustice in my opinion.

This book will entertain, but hopefully also enlighten those fans who, like me eight years ago, felt they knew Jamie. In truth the man behind the myth is more of a champion than he ever was on the field.

James Deighton
Rugby League producer, BBC Radio Leeds

About the author

Andrew Hardcastle is a retired schoolteacher, married with two grown-up children. He had to play rugby union at school and college, but grew up with rugby league, both amateur and professional. He became connected with Halifax RLFC, where he has been club historian for 30 years, timekeeper and one-time occasional second team player. He has contributed to a variety of publications, magazines and newspapers, writing mostly on rugby league.
His previous books have been:
The Thrum Hall Story, a history of Halifax RLFC, 1986.
They played for Halifax, 1987
Halifax at Wembley, 1987.
Thrum Hall Greats, 1994.
Halifax Rugby League, The First Hundred Years, Tempus, 1998.
Lost, the former cricket clubs and grounds of Halifax and Calderdale, Cricket Heritage Project, 2006.
Garfield Owen – Rugby Footballer, 2010 (London League Publications Ltd)

Thank you

London League Publications Ltd would like to thank Steve McCarthy for designing the jacket, David Williams of rlphotos.com for the photos for the jacket, other photographers as credited and the staff of Charlesworth Press for printing the book.

Introduction: Arrest nightmare

Just as this book was originally about to go to print in the summer of 2012, a story appeared in *The Sun* that Jamie had been arrested. It was explosive stuff, with the insinuation of a sexual offence with a child. "Rugby league ace Jamie Bloem in 'child sex' cop quiz" screamed the headline, with an accompanying photograph from his time as a player. The story was repeated in other newspapers, and covered on radio news bulletins, with devastating consequences.

As well as the effect on his reputation, he received death threats, his business suffered, his progress as a referee was put on hold, and his life seemed wrecked.

To those who knew him, it all appeared so unlikely. In the course of writing the book, I had come to know him quite well. He is clearly a happily married man with two great kids. If the accusation had been that he had punched someone, I could have thought back to his rugby career and might have believed there could be some truth in it. But this just did not ring true. It always seemed more likely just to be the latest in a long line of press reports, covered later in the book, that have accused him over the years of this, that or the other, making him out to be something different from what he really is, and that have usually turned out to be well wide of the mark. To have his name published under such headlines seemed utterly unfair. As Dave Larder, a former Halifax playing colleague, tweeted when he was cleared: "Don't think that any person who knew him ever doubted his innocence."

Now that everything is over, he is keen to consign it to the past, but is pleased to have the opportunity to set the record straight. He has done this partially in local and national press interviews, and also on television and radio, but can now reveal the full story.

The report in *The Sun* was a shock to Jamie, coming 10 days after he had indeed been interviewed by police. That in itself was a bolt from the blue. It was early on the morning of 4 July that the police arrived.

"I heard a knock on the door," he remembers, "and found two detectives standing there, with two further uniformed officers at the gate, a police car behind them and another car with a blue light on the other side of the road. They asked to come in, but the two in uniform stayed outside the house in full view of my neighbours. They came in and asked whether anyone else was in the house, and I said that my wife Louise was upstairs helping our daughter get ready for school.

When Louise and Isabelle departed, I was told I was being arrested for having sex with a minor. Shock set in straight away then; I went numb. They asked if I knew the minor involved – and I did. Then they asked for everything that could receive internet communication, and I handed over my computers, together with my MacBook, iPad, iPod and my iPhone. I was taken to Halifax police station, while the two detectives stayed in the house to search it. Louise arrived home to find them in the kitchen bagging up the computers." She was told that Jamie had been arrested, but left to fret with little other information.

He was locked up for a time, interviewed, and released on bail at 5pm, though the police held on to his computers and phones. It was a tough time for him in the cells, worrying about how he could prove his innocence, and about what the police might have told Louise. "You go through ways of trying to save yourself, even though you haven't done anything wrong."

The police were responding to notification from Facebook that an inappropriate act might have taken place. This stemmed from an unofficial social event at Stainland amateur rugby league club, where Jamie was player-coach at the time, following their achievement of promotion from Division 4 of the Pennine League in March. Unbeknown to the committee, a party was held, attended by around 15 blokes and five girls, but not including Jamie. One of the criticisms he received at clubs was that he left soon after the games. "Stainland didn't like that a lot," says Jamie, "but Saturday nights for me are family time. That night I went with Louise to La Luna restaurant in Halifax. I have the receipts and credit card record." Meanwhile, photographs taken at the Stainland gathering, some of them quite revealing, were posted on Facebook, with equally graphic comments. Jamie was then tagged in to the photographs, which made him appear a part of what had happened. The fact that he was older than the others, and that a couple of the girls turned out to be only 15 years old, became an issue, and was reported by Facebook.

"I knew the two girls from them being at matches," admits Jamie. "They weren't strangers. They had told me they were 17, in their final year at school. They were each a 'friend' on Facebook. When they had requested me as a "friend", I thought nothing of it. Our conversations on the site had nothing untoward in them from my point of view, though the police were suspicious and found some things that they thought were pertinent to the case. I actually discovered in April that one of the girls was 15, put on a message saying so, and defriended her, which helped me with the police eventually. Social media sites have protection in place for children, which is great, but there's none for adults. People should have to prove their identity as part of the registration process, so the wider public know if they are a minor."

In early May Jamie left for a family holiday in Gran Canaria with Louise and the kids, unaware there was any problem. "We were sending photographs back via Facebook, but half-way through Facebook closed down. It had been hacked before, so I thought it was the same and set up another. I didn't think anything of it."

All this time the police investigation was going on, leading to the July arrest. The Facebook evidence seemed to them incriminating. Although he was not in the Stainland pictures, the police had a suspicion that he might have been the one taking them. The pictures were removed from Facebook after a week at the police's request, but Jamie's account was being monitored. "The police came to my home to arrest someone they saw as a paedophile. But I co-operated fully with them and told them what I knew. I think they soon realised I wasn't involved in the way they first thought I was. By the time of the second interview they had calmed right down." The allegations of sex with a minor were dropped; the bail sheet now referred to a lesser charge of contact with a minor.

He might not have appreciated at the time the way the police had gone about things or the accusations they made, but he accepts they had to investigate the complaint they had received. "I understand that the police had a job to do. For every person like me who is innocent, there will be others who are guilty. What I was initially accused of is a heinous crime. People who prey on young girls are the core hate of everyone in the civilised world. To be tarred with that brush was terrible." While in the cells, he saw and heard how much the police have to put up with. "People were kicking off, shouting and swearing at them for just doing their jobs. They actually treated me very well, with dignity and respect, and gave me a cell out of the way where I wouldn't be seen by the public. Then, after finger-printing and DNA etc, I got a different cell, with a toilet."

Knowing that he had done nothing wrong helped. The girl involved had said there was no contact, and the episode seemed to be fading away. But the opposite was about to unfold when it all became public knowledge.

Just over a week later, *The Sun* got hold of the story and published it with the original charge, naming him and suddenly making everyone aware of his arrest. In no time at all it was all over the internet – on Facebook, the rugby league message boards, and further afield. "Half of the places where the news was being reported don't even play rugby league. They wouldn't even know who I was." It seemed a photographer had been taking pictures of his kids playing outside, and reporters knocking on his neighbours' doors asking how they felt about him living close to their children.

That was when the nightmare really started. For the next three months, until he was released from police bail with all allegations dropped and no further action being taken, the lives of Jamie and his family were turned upside down. He had to face the horror that people might believe it was actually true, as some certainly did. On the Saturday morning the news broke, the family left for a pre-arranged trip to his mother's home in Middlesbrough, but Jamie returned alone for work on the Monday to find a threatening message left on his answerphone. It was followed by a letter with death threats, saying what the writer wanted to do to him and his daughter, in quite explicit terms. He contacted the police, who advised that the rest of the family should remain at his mother's. It was two or three weeks before the family felt there was no longer a risk; that the messages were from mindless idiots having fun at their expense.

Things did not get any easier. There was the possibility that national press coverage might escalate when fresh allegations were made to the police of further involvement with one of the girls, with claims that he had met up with her on seven occasions. However, his solicitor warned the reporter that his newspaper would be liable if the allegations were shown to be false, and the story never appeared. Fortunately, Jamie was able to provide alibis to the police on all of the dates to discredit the new story. Sometimes it was his refereeing appointments that served to prove he was elsewhere.

One was the Saturday evening before he took charge of Workington Town versus Gateshead on the Sunday, when phone records proved that Ian Smith, his RFL manager as a referee, had rung to talk about the match at the relevant time. For another he could show he was officiating Leeds versus Warrington under-20s at Stanningley, and one of the others he was in London for the Broncos versus Castleford under-20s curtain-raiser to the Super League fixture between the same clubs. "I travelled down with Phil Bentham, George Stokes and the other officials for both matches, all in one car, and we were staying over at the Marriot Hotel in Twickenham at the time I was accused of being somewhere else." A 1 April meeting was claimed to have been in his brand new car, but he had not bought it until 14 April, and for another date, he had parking receipts to show he was visiting Louise in hospital. Louise has developed a number of medical problems in recent years, including only 20 per cent function of her kidneys.

The press coverage, even without these additions, had been intrusive enough. "For a while I was too scared to go out of the house, embarrassed that people would be thinking I'd done something." People cancelled bookings for his landscaping business, saying they were uncomfortable having him working for them. It left him with financial difficulties, because he was already without income from his rugby league refereeing and his radio commentary work. "The nature of the case meant that all the bodies I am affiliated with, like the RFL and BBC, had to be informed, and temporary bans were put on me."

Both organisations remained very supportive though. The BBC gave him the chance to explain to the general public once he was cleared, and the RFL stood by him, notably Ian Smith and match officials director Stuart Cummings. Jamie recalls: "Stuart was fantastic and told me to keep going. Ian telephoned me twice every week in the very beginning, and once every week after that, just to check on my state of mind and encouraging me to keep myself fit."

Regrettably for Jamie, social services were required to be called in. "They came to my house and interviewed me, my wife and daughter. Being asked whether I posed a risk to my daughter has to be the hardest thing in all of this. But social services have a very difficult job, and I don't for one minute blame them for coming in there with a very stern attitude. I explained the case to them and they softened up."

It was obviously a difficult time for his son and daughter, Jordan and Isabelle. Telling them what was going on was tough to do, assuring them that he had done nothing wrong and that it would eventually all go away. "Isabelle's school has been fantastic. I am involved with the Parent Teachers Association there, and went in to speak to the head and deputy head. They told me to keep my head up and said they would sort out the gossipers. Jordan's high school was the same. They watched and monitored him, and I can't thank them enough for what they have done for him."

Lots of others were very supportive. The threatening messages were vastly outnumbered by those backing him. It was a worry what other people would be thinking about him after reading the sensationalised reports, but these helped. "We go to church on a Sunday and the people there have been fantastic, when they could easily have turned their backs on me." And wife Louise was there for him as she always had been in the past, standing by him all along. "There are many wives who I'm sure wouldn't have done that," he admits, "whether the allegations were true or false. On the day I was arrested I walked home from the police station in the pouring rain. She wasn't happy. 'Do I need to know anything?' she asked. But I said 'Do you think I would do that?' She has never asked me again."

Finally, in October, he was cleared, a tremendous relief and release. "There might still be people who think I've got away with something just because I had a good solicitor. But it was just a duty solicitor, Joanne from Goodwin Stevens in Halifax, who happened to be very good. She told me she wasn't used to defending innocent people." Although the sleepless nights have not completely gone away, the torment is passing now and he is able to get on with his life again, including publishing this biography. Initial thoughts of suing newspapers and people who spilled the story have faded and, though he reckons he has lost thousands of pounds, his income is returning to normal. New CRB checks for both the Rugby Football League and the Rugby Football Union were clear, so refereeing appointments were back, and he resumed his playing career. While he had enjoyed his time at Stainland, and had nothing but respect for Gary Ellis, the official who bought him to the club, chairman John Sutcliffe and the others, it was time to move on. He decided to rejoin Old Rishworthians RUFC, just as a player, when refereeing commitments allowed. Coach Damian Ball, another former Halifax rugby league player, was eager to have him involved in a Yorkshire Three promotion and championship push.

The experience has changed him slightly. "I'm more reserved in what I say now," he admits. "And I didn't play Santa this last Christmas, at the school or in the neighbourhood, as I had normally done in the past. That upsets me as much as anything. There are some things I can't do now."

Being in the sporting limelight had on this occasion worked against him. The incident would not have merited a mention in the national press in the first place had it not been for his name as a rugby league referee and player.

His rise to prominence as a sportsman, which the book is mainly about, had itself been extraordinary. Until he was 20 years old, Jamie had never even heard of rugby league. A similar length of time later he had become a front line Super League star, international, referee, commentator and coach in it.

Brought up in the apartheid regime of South Africa, his is a remarkable story of disputes, battles with authority, controversy and sporting highs and lows.

Wherever he played, no matter how successful he became on the field, there was always a knock-back around the corner. From fall-outs with rugby union selectors in South Africa, to drug issues at Doncaster, arguments with Halifax officials, and now a Facebook scandal, he has kept going and overcome the adversity. His is a fascinating story.

Andrew Hardcastle
January 2013

Acknowledgements

This book was built around a series of interviews at Jamie's home. He was always open and forthcoming, and he and Louise the most welcoming of hosts.

Background information on Halifax RLFC came from my records, but for his other clubs I am grateful for help from Roger Halstead (Oldham), Deb Townsend (Widnes) and David Gronow (Huddersfield) and the Old Rishworthians RFC website. My thanks to Gerry Wright of Bradford, a reliable source for rugby league information. The various rugby league yearbooks provided statistics, as did *The British Rugby League Records Book.*

Jamie had extensive scrapbooks of press cuttings, though sometimes the names of the publications from which they came were absent. His collection of photographs was not as wide, and I am grateful to Keith Hamer, Mike Riley, Darrell Cooper, David Williams (rlphotos.com) and the *Halifax Evening Courier* for their help in this area.

My thanks to David Garforth, Laura Fairbank at the RFL, Maureen Juniper from the Yorkshire RFU and Halifax RLFC chairman Michael Steele who checked the Halifax sections for accuracy.

Andrew Hardcastle

Contents

Jamie and Louise.

Thanks and dedications

Throughout my career, I have met and got to know many fantastic and inspirational people. It would take too long to thank each of them individually, so this is to them all.

But special thanks go out to June and Peter Baker at Doncaster. Without them I would have probably turned my back on rugby league and returned home to South Africa. They took me in at my lowest point and made me realise what I would be missing out on. I could never thank them enough.

I would like to make the following dedications for this book:

First, my mum and dad: They provided me with all the correct tools to be successful in life, and had to put up with me growing up!! My biggest compliment to them is, we never had a lot, but never wanted for anything.

Second is my beautiful wife Louise. She is battling a crippling bone disease and kidney failure, but wakes up every morning with a huge smile on her face, and soldiers through her own pain to look after me and our kids. Without her I wouldn't be half the person I am today. She is an inspiration, my true love and my best friend.

And lastly, all the rugby league fans past and present who have stood by me, chanted for and against me, and made me feel special... just for a little while. Thank you, and enjoy my story.

Jamie Bloem
January 2013

1. Drugs shame

"I know 12 players in the game who if they were tested tomorrow would be positive for anabolic steroids. I have played in matches where players have taken steroids."

These were just two of the startling claims made by Jamie Bloem in January 1995. They appeared in the *Mail on Sunday* when his agent negotiated a deal with the newspaper following Jamie's own two-year drugs ban a few weeks earlier.

He went on to add that "Players are offered steroids and take them. The Rugby League says I'm an isolated case and that's rubbish. I'll guarantee you now that if the Rugby League went and tested ten players from each team playing at the moment, they would find it very hard to get full sides out on the field. Blind eyes have been turned everywhere."

The Rugby Football League authorities reacted strongly to the accusations, Chief Executive Maurice Lindsay blasting his claims that drug taking was rife in the sport. "I dismiss these comments as the rantings of a disgraced athlete who was discovered to be taking steroids by the league's random testing system. He is nothing less than a disgraced, lying cheat." Jamie was ordered to Chapeltown Road and told to retract his statements. "I asked them if they were telling me to lie, but they said I had no way of substantiating what I was saying."

They were quite correct; he could not prove what he was saying and he was not about to start naming names. His words had been those of an angry boy, stimulated when the reporter visited, along with a colleague to do a photo-shoot. The threat of a life ban persuaded him to agree to the retraction.

But he had not been making it up. "Most of the Doncaster players were taking something during my second season there in 1994–95," he remembers. "It's why we kept winning games." His personal involvement was unconnected with any team-mate, a personal arrangement with a guy at the gym to cure an injury, and it was not a topic that was ever openly discussed, but he knew it was happening. Many were on Winstrel, a water-based hormone also used on racehorses, which would be in and out of the system in a couple of days.

1

Andy Gregory, then playing for Salford, distanced himself from Jamie when interviewed by Paul Harrison in *The Sun* soon after the original allegations in 1995, but did acknowledge that drugs were being used. "Let's not kid ourselves," he said. "Rugby League does have a drug problem. It's not as widespread as some people claim, but I believe there are those around who take anabolic steroids to build up muscle and bulk... We have got to stamp out the use of drugs now before it becomes rife."

Players in any sport have always tried to find ways to improve their performance, traditionally through simple things like diet – a surfeit of eggs or steak maybe. By the 1960s and 1970s a few mysterious pills and potions had entered the mix, though the players might have had little idea of what they contained, which would probably have been nothing illegal, and would only have used them rarely.

Drugs like steroids were relatively new in 1994. Amphetamine, a psychostimulant drug which produces increased focus along with a reduction in fatigue, began to be produced in the 1930s and was widely used by soldiers during the Second World War, but it was the 1950s before the Soviets began to use male hormones and the Americans responded with steroids.

Drug testing was even more recent. It had begun at the Mexico City Olympics in 1968, but had not spread to other sports until later. Rugby League was one of the first to introduce it in 1987. By 1994 there had been no positive tests in League for steroids, though there had been some for other substances. Bradford Northern forward Simon Tuffs had been banned for two years in 1991 after testing positive for amphetamines, but it had been lifted after a subsequent police investigation, Halifax's Dave Watson had been suspended for three months in 1992 for cannabis, and Great Britain's Graham Steadman fined and warned after the 1992 Tour for pseudo-ephedrine, a cold remedy. On the same day as Jamie was banned, Barrie Ledger, Swinton's former Great Britain winger, tested positive for traces of cannabis. Many other sports fared worse, and tested less.

"Drugs are probably still a problem today," surmised Jamie recently. "Where money is an incentive, some will always try to break the rules. I don't want to sound like a hypocrite, but there are no excuses nowadays. People know about drugs now. Not that I necessarily blame the players. Thirty-five or more games a season is tough, the extra

2

game over the Easter weekend was hard, so they are just looking to supplement themselves. There probably needs to be even more testing." Jamie knew little about drugs as a youngster, but playing Rugby Union in South Africa in the early 1990s he had come across Reactivan. This was an aspirin-based tablet, a stimulant developed in the 1960s, which increased drive and mental alertness, and was regarded as safe. "Everyone was taking it," recalls Jamie, in an accent still clearly revealing his Afrikaans descent. "I did too. I didn't know any better."

Then, in 1992, a South African prop forward died from it, suffering a heart attack on the field. It thinned the blood, and in his case caused his heart to beat so fast that it effectively burst. There was a consequent clampdown, with 10 players banned for steroid use and eight more for stimulants over the next five or six years.

Jamie had left for England in 1992 though, and knew nothing of this. Drugs never crossed his mind, and were never seen, when playing at Castleford and Oldham, or at Doncaster either when he first arrived there. It later became apparent, however, that some Doncaster players were taking what turned out to be performance-enhancing steroids, which were originating from one of the Lancashire-based players. One team-mate quickly changed from producing short bursts to being able to last the full 80 minutes, while another was smoking cannabis. "I knew they were doing things, but I didn't know exactly what."

His own introduction to drugs was somewhat accidental, and unconnected with improving performance. During the off-season after Doncaster's promotion to the top division in 1993, he developed a problem with his hernia, first at one side, then the other tore as well. It was an exciting time for the team, and he was keen to be involved, but the club had already paid for operations for other squad members and were not keen to fund another.

Doncaster RLFC had their own physiotherapist, but there was no strengthening coach – they used the people employed by the gym where they often trained; it was they who provided them with fitness programmes. One of these suggested that a couple of injections every other week for five weeks or so would cure the problem, and at the same time make him stronger. They were not particularly expensive, about £20 a time, and there was no mention of what the injections contained. It seemed a good idea.

"I didn't for one minute think of it as doing anything illegal," remembers Jamie, who was still a relative youngster. "I was pumped up to play, and had just signed a new two-year contract. I was earning big money and things were looking good. The injections were to clear up the double hernia, not for performance enhancing." The injury duly healed, he was feeling fine, and putting on immense amounts of muscle weight. Although he didn't know what was in the injections, he did now become suspicious, but had no qualms about adding pills to the regime in the weeks between the injections. He later found that the injected drug was Decadon, which regrows muscle. The tablets were Dianabol, also a testosterone-based anabolic steroid. They served to reduce the recovery time for his muscles, so he could do more work on a daily basis, which transformed his physique in a short time.

He got big, growing from around 13 and a half stone to 15 and a half quickly, such that his clothes were no longer fitting well. "I felt like a superhero!" The last injection was two weeks into the season, but he carried on with the tablets. "I suppose part of me liked what it was doing; I was playing out of my skin."

The first match of the season was away to St Helens, a formidable start to life in the top league – Saints had splashed out nearly half a million pounds on the likes of Bobbie Goulding and Scott Gibbs over the summer break. Raymond Fletcher, in his *Yorkshire Post* match preview, wrote that if sentiment counted for anything Doncaster's first season in Division One would be a guaranteed success as everybody was wishing the once perennial strugglers good luck. "The hard facts, however, are reflected in the bookmakers' odds which offer them up at 2000–1 for the title."

Team-mate Vila Matautia, in an interview with Ian Bridge in 2001, remembered the match well. "It was one of the most memorable games in Doncaster history," he recalled. "We were never given a rat's chance in hell. But Jamie Bloem ripped in for two devastating tries."

Jamie felt unstoppable, aggressive and fast. One of his tries came straight from a 20-metre tap-restart when he ran past Adam Fogerty and ended up outsprinting Anthony Sullivan to the tryline. "Normally I was reasonably quick, but I was never gifted with great pace like Sullivan." Vila Matautia, Audley Pennant and Sonny Whakarau also crossed as the Dons won 29–20.

"Doncaster produced possibly the finest display in their 43 year history to record an astonishing upset over title hopefuls St Helens," enthused the *Yorkshire Post* match report. "Inspired by full-back Jamie Bloem and talented half-back Alex Green, Doncaster outplayed their big spending rivals in every department." In describing the tries, it wrote that "Bloem gave Doncaster a dream start... when he raced 80 metres for a stunning opening score in the eighth minute", that "the elusive South African grabbed his second just before the break", that "in the second half Bloem's 40-metre break was halted on half-way, but Brendan Carlisle and winger Mark Roache carved an opening for Audley Pennant to cross", and that "Bloem split Saints defence once more in the final minute and second row forward Vila Matautia sealed an historic win."

At home to Widnes the following week on Sky Sports there were two more tries for him in a 21–6 triumph, as Doncaster hit the top of the table. "There were many outstanding performances last night," wrote Raymond Fletcher on Saturday 27 August, "but Jamie Bloem repeated his two-try display at St Helens to take the home man of the match award. The South African full-back looked unstoppable at times and crashed through for a solo try in each half."

There was a downside to all this however. Jamie's main memory of the Widnes match was not of the tries, but of shoving David Ruane into the television equipment on the side-line. He had always been an aggressive player, but now this was going to extremes. He did much the same in the next match against Leeds, the first defeat of the season. Barrie McDermott, a former team-mate at Oldham but by this time a Leeds player, wrote in his autobiography, "I remember his barging full back Alan Tait off the pitch and into a stone post," leaving him in need of stitches. "It was pure aggression," recalls Jamie. "I didn't feel bad about it at the time, though I do now. There was no remorse, I'd become a person I didn't like."

Away from the field, he suffered quite vicious mood swings – fine one minute then losing his temper. He had just started dating Doncaster girl Louise Britten, his future wife who worked at the gym the players used. Obviously she noticed and asked what was going on, but there was no escape from his anger. "I'd get angry at the smallest thing."

Tackled by Patrick Entat and James Lowes in Doncaster's match against Leeds at Tattersfield in September 1994. Ellery Hanley closes in. The Doncaster players are Sonny Whakarau on the left and Brendan Carlisle.

Jamie races clear of Scott Gibbs, as Ian Fletcher and Tony Bowes look on in Doncaster's famous win at Knowsley Road in 1994.

After beating Wakefield Trinity, where he was sin-binned for use of the elbow in a tackle, Doncaster travelled to Oldham in mid-September. After 13 minutes, loose forward Mike Kuiti broke through for Oldham and Jamie hit him high after he had off-loaded a try-scoring pass to Gary Lord, damaging his jaw. Referee Steve Cross brought out the red card on the intervention of a touch judge, and Oldham went on to win convincingly. Jamie put on his track-suit and walked out of Watersheddings – and didn't stop. "I carried on walking, up Saddleworth Road, over the moors, along the M62 towards Doncaster. I was eventually given a lift by a Doncaster supporter, but couldn't remember how I'd got there – somewhere near Birstall I think."

Alarm bells started ringing for Jamie. "I was losing my mind big time. I didn't feel bad about smacking Mike Kuiti. He's a lovely fella, and I used to play for Oldham, but I wanted to hit him. It was worrying. I can understand completely what Terry Newton must have gone through before he committed suicide. Luckily I had people who stood by me. I told the guy at the gym I didn't want any more tablets, that if he came after me with them again I would go to the police."

He was given a three match suspension for the sending off, missing matches against Warrington, Salford and Halifax. All were lost, the latter at Tattersfield by 72–0 as Halifax ran riot, John Schuster notching 32 points with 10 goals and three tries.

Jamie was back for the following week's game against Castleford, and with dramatic effect. "Jamie Bloem was the toast of Tattersfield as Doncaster sensationally turned the form book upside down," reported one of the national newspapers. "Bloem returned after suspension to lift the spirits of a demoralised Doncaster side... notching a dazzling hat-trick of tries with an inspired display that left Castleford shell-shocked." He was the *Doncaster Star* man of the match, leaving him clear of the field in the race to win their new Starman Award, having amassed 18 points out of a possible 45.

After a trip to Workington, and a narrow 19–16 defeat, next up were St Helens, smarting after Doncaster's earlier win on their ground. Saints star Bobbie Goulding came into the changing rooms before the match to announce that the drugs testers were there, and that anyone who was on something had better not play. "You should drop out," he said pointedly to Jamie. The Doncaster lads felt Bobbie was saying this to weaken their side, and told him to leave. Saints won anyway, 24–5,

7

and Jamie was duly chosen for testing. The Rugby League authorities deny he was targeted, but Bobby Goulding knew and it must have been obvious from the way he was playing. He later heard that Doncaster had been told player numbers 1 and 12 would be selected.

With these being the early days of drugs testing, the implications might not have been fully appreciated, not by Jamie certainly, but some realised the difficulty he was in. One of the backroom staff gave him a condom filled with urine. "Put this in your trousers, "he said, "and when you get in there break it open as you give the sample." Then on the toilet was a note. "Look under the bowl." There was a cup there from one of the players, filled with another sample.

It could not happen nowadays, when the testers watch directly, but there was ample opportunity to use either of these. This particular tester sent Jamie into a cubicle, while he himself stayed outside filling in various forms. But whether through not realising the illegality of the substances he had taken, or maybe looking back subconsciously wanting to be caught, he provided a legitimate sample.

Within a few days he was called to a meeting at Rugby League Headquarters at Chapeltown Road for the afternoon of Tuesday 29 November, "to discuss the test". In the meantime he had appeared for Doncaster at Leeds, where according to Ray French "his hard-hitting two-try performance ... did much to elevate him into second position behind St Helens No 1 Steve Prescott, is *Open Rugby* magazine's ratings for full-backs this month." [*]

Leeds had shown interest in him before and his performance renewed it. An offer came in from Dougie Laughton to take him to Headingley on a contract of £2,000 per week, with Doncaster receiving a £150,000 transfer fee. The plan further included a summer spell with Malcolm Reilly's Newcastle Knights in Australia, worth "a lot of money". Jamie went over to meet them on the Tuesday morning, and while players Ellery Hanley and Gary Schofield convinced him of the merits of joining Leeds, the chairman and his agent reached agreement and the forms were signed. He was suddenly a Leeds player.

In the afternoon it was off to Chapeltown Road for his meeting – nothing too serious it seemed. However, details had been leaked to the press, the car park being filled with reporters to whom he innocently chatted. Jamie had not been told that it was a formal hearing, and was

---

[*] *Today*, November 1994

unrepresented, but RFL chief executive Maurice Lindsay was present with chairman Rodney Walker and a RFL solicitor. Sample A had proved positive for Nandrolone, the first such finding in rugby league. There was also evidence of testosterone. He was asked if he would like to have the Sample B tested himself. "I didn't see the need," says Jamie. "It was the same sample and would produce the same results, so there didn't seem much point."

The officials took that as an admission of guilt, which in effect it was, so within two or three minutes the meeting was over and he was asked to wait outside. A few more seconds passed and he was called back for the verdict, a two-year ban. It was the maximum sentence for a first offence under the game's by-laws. He questioned the lack of representation, but was told that was not important, and was given 28 days to appeal. The test had shown incredibly high amounts in his system – dangerously high levels he was told – so he chose not to exercise his option.

With the press still outside, he was offered the opportunity to leave by the rear emergency exit, where a taxi was waiting to take him back to Doncaster. Back home, he phoned Louise to suggest she would be better finding someone else, though she offered her full support. He also phoned Doug Laughton, who said that the Leeds contract would have to be cancelled as though it had never happened. The Doncaster contract was terminated too, chairman John Desmond asking him to drop off his club car the following day.

His agent Derek Parker wanted initially to fight the case, but backed off when Jamie told him the full story. "Jamie is very upset," he told the press. "He doesn't take drugs on a regular basis. It was a mistake and he accepts the decision. He is full of remorse for what he has done." Parker was at least able to secure him his club car for a further six weeks, though the rent Doncaster RLFC paid for his home stopped immediately. Luckily his landlord was a Doncaster fan, who allowed him to stay on for another couple of months free of charge.

Many were quite scathing. Maurice Lindsay, interviewed by Phil Hodgson in the *Rugby Leaguer* weekly newspaper dated 5 December, seemed to direct the blame at the fact Jamie was South African. "I understand that there have been many positive drug-testings in South African rugby union," he is quoted as saying. "Maybe the attitude to drugs in that country is different to elsewhere, perhaps their long period of isolation has led them down the wrong path." He was sure that there were no other cases. "Of the thousands tested since 1987, this is the first positive steroid testing and it so happens it's arisen when a South African has come over here to play our game and has been caught, and he will have to accept our punishment."

There was a hint of sympathy when he added. "Jamie Bloem, the poor lad, has created tremendous difficulties for himself because he's now unable to earn money with Doncaster, so he'll have no income, and it therefore follows that his work permit will be under threat." Jamie did not need a work permit; he held a British passport because his mother was Scottish. But Maurice Lindsay's views connecting it with him being South African was annoying. "It was like I'd been doing it over there and had come over to infect his game," he complains.

Elsewhere in the same newspaper, Mike Stephenson in his column *Stevo* went further, and called for a life ban: "Ban them for life!" he wrote. "We should not mess about with any player caught cheating or taking anabolic steroids. One has to applaud the bosses at Chapeltown Road for kicking out Doncaster's Jamie Bloem for that particular offence. But it would have had more impact if they had slung him out of the game forever."

Great Britain star Jonathan Davies, quoted in the *Today* newspaper, followed a similar hard line. "Bloem knew the risks. There are pressures on players to improve their physique. But they must stay within the laws. Two years seems lenient." Like Stephenson, he was assuming the steroids were to build him up and make him a better player, which was not quite the case.

The implications of what he had done did not sink in straight away. Two years can seem like an eternity when looking forward, but that was not how he felt at first. He could talk about it, sleep well enough, and think about appealing the severity of the sanction. After a few days though, once he had been sacked without even receiving the wages he had earned the previous week, the feeling hit that he suddenly had no prospects, no future over here, no future in rugby league, and no future with Louise. "I left for three weeks, went to stay with a mate, sleeping on his settee," he regrets. "This mate didn't have a job either. I'm not a drinker, but we went out on benders. I was on a downward spiral, felt victimised, full of self-pity."

Louise's mother was highly critical of his drug-taking, but saw how it was affecting her daughter and managed to get in touch with him to invite him round for tea. "He'd disappeared," says Louise. "He didn't answer his phone. I was devastated. But then he accepted mum's invitation." From that point things started to look up. Louise had no hesitation in offering her full backing. Indeed, it was the support he received in general at this time that saw him through and prevented the sort of situation that Terry Newton found himself in 16 years later.

Louise was there for him. "We'll get through this together," she told him. The pair sat down and had a long talk about it, Louise being adamant that she did not wish to cut ties. Then there was his sponsor at Doncaster, Peter Baker, who with his wife June and teenage daughters Kerry and Shelley, took Jamie into his home. The girls moved to share a bedroom, leaving one for him. When he later asked that Louise move in too, that was accepted without question. "I still send June a card each Mothers' Day," says a grateful Jamie.

He organised a garage sale to get rid of his stuff. Some Doncaster friends, Jackie and Rob and daughter Gail who lived nearby, helped out, advertising it in the *Doncaster Free Press* and *Doncaster Star*, and producing leaflets. The place was packed, the police arriving to help manage the crowds, and everything went – television, fish tank, the whole lot –apart from the stuff he wanted to keep, which he had to put in the car. By evening the house was clear and he had some £9,000 in a tin. "Someone offered £50 for a pile of washing!"

Rob was manager of the pub soccer team at the Black Bull, Jamie having played in goal for them when rugby commitments allowed. Now he was able to play for them every Sunday. "We were a good team. In the summer we played cricket as well, 25-over stuff on Wednesday nights. It was great fun." Jamie was a decent cricketer, having played earlier for Pegler's in the Doncaster League – Pegler's were the Dons shirt sponsors – and later for Warley, Northowram Hedge Top and Copley in the Halifax League. "I love cricket. I play it like I play rugby. I hit the ball as hard as I can with my heavy bat, and get either quick runs or nothing." He is also a medium-pace change bowler. "I can swing it in the air, though I don't know how."

Now he had options and could be positive again. Peter Baker gave him a job. He was a plumber, and took Jamie on as an apprentice, paying him £20 a day on top of his lodgings.

American Football training – Jamie is number 66.

They also had Louise's income from the gym too. Plus there was a handy little deal from the press. Many of the nationals, being staunchly behind rugby union, loved any story that would shed league in a bad light. Hearing of Jamie's assertions that loads of other league players were taking drugs, the *Mail on Sunday* paid him £25,000 for his story. Not that he ended up with the full amount. Agent Derek Parker took a £5,000 chunk, and then the newspaper demanded a 50 per cent refund when he had to retract some of the allegations. "I had to give them £12,500, which was way more than half of what I'd received. I don't recall my agent repaying anything. That's agents for you!"

Some of what was left was used to buy into a mate's decorating business. "He had a contract for Gala Bingo Halls, and we went down to London to wallpaper a flat belonging to Shirley Bassey, though she wasn't there; we used 400 rolls of 24 carat leaf gold paper at £399 a roll. I wasn't earning much from it though, being used a bit I think, and pulled out to go back to the plumbing. I didn't get all my stake back."

The emotional seesaw was back up again when he joined South Yorkshire Jaguars, a local amateur American Football side, for the 1995 season. "I played running back – my rugby background made me decent at it, though it was very different. The games lasted about five hours, with barbecues going on along the sidelines, though with all the stoppages you're only actually playing about 30 minutes." He made such a success of it – he still figures in the All-time British American Football records in 13th spot for 'most yards rushing' – that a scout with the professional London Monarchs side asked him to join their

The Bakers at Jordan's christening in Doncaster.

feeder team, London Olympians. "Some of the guys were huge; to me they seemed juiced up. They weren't a bit bothered that I had the ban for steroids."

He was offered a massive contract with the Monarchs. At the time, they competed with five other European-based teams in a World League, based at the White Hart Lane ground of Tottenham Hotspur Football Club. They had earlier used Wembley Stadium, famously recruiting Ellery Hanley, though he never played. Most of the Monarchs players were young Americans assigned from National Football League sides, but the rules required the participation of at least one player of European extraction.

Jamie would also have been a more than useful kicker, a role he had taken sometimes with the Jaguars. "But I couldn't see myself playing the game professionally. With all the armour, the hits were huge and placed a tremendous strain on your knees. They also expected me to move to London. Louise didn't fancy that, so we turned it down. It helped keeping my spirits up though, being wanted again."

Thanks largely to Louise's wages, they were able to get a flat together at Carcroft, followed by a semi at Woodlands, three miles north of Doncaster.

Watching the local Woodlands amateur rugby league team in action landed him in trouble again though. He was invited to play for a Woodlands Select XIII in a charity match to raise funds for a local child who was poorly, so the kid could have a special operation. "I couldn't see a problem with that, so I played. The day raised around £2,500." But then he was ordered to appear before amateur rugby league chief executive Maurice Oldroyd at BARLA headquarters. "The insinuation was that I had played in a league game for Woodlands 'A', and I was banned for six months. It was worth it because of the money I had helped raise. I wasn't bothered about a ban when I was already banned."

Life was good again, and plans could be made to a return to professional rugby league.

2. More than just a nutter

Jamie has always had a reputation for aggressive play. "People have often thought of me as a rugby-playing nutter," he says. It made him popular with his own team's fans if not the opposition's. He was a South Stand hero in his time at The Shay with Halifax, and was similarly a crowd favourite at his other clubs. Doncaster fans likened his attitude and hairstyle to that of soccer hard-man of the period Vinny Jones, "I like to class myself as an entertainer, to get the crowd going and talk to them during the game," he told reporter Steve Fox while with Widnes.

When he first started getting involved with rugby as a youngster, his dad's advice was that he should come off the field at the end of a game with the opposition players and supporters hating him. He greatly respected his dad, so that was how he played – never taking a backward step, and mixing it. "I was always passionate. When you go on the field you're challenging yourself. I always play with my heart on my sleeve. If you are going to play in a friendly way, you might as well be playing in the park with your mates. It's a pride thing with me. I hate to lose. I like to play it a bit rough." He is not in favour of players running to the referee to complain about being hurt. "The professional game's not for babies and girls."

His playing weight settled at around 100 kilograms, just over 15 stones, and his height at 6 feet 1 inch. Not the biggest, but enough to give him plenty of physicality. Some saw him as a dirty player, but it was not quite like that. "He always played hard," comments Halifax team-mate Martin Moana. "He gave a bit of stick here and there; he was fiery more than anything." He got a bit back of course, as his mum quickly discovered when she watched him play. "I cringed sometimes," she says. "I thought, 'Oh God, they've killed him!'"

This image as a player is very different to how he comes across off the field. Like many similar rugby league players, in everyday life he is unrecognisable as the same person. For one thing, he inherited some of his mum's artistic side, becoming South Africa's under–10s figure-skating champion at the age of five or six, and doing ballet for many years. "I was fearless," he says of the figure-skating, "so tried things that others wouldn't and got marked up for it."

15

BBC Radio Leeds commentator James Deighton, a close friend, makes the same observation about his image: "Over the years I have come to know a man who couldn't be further away from his reputation on the field. Through his radio work I'm delighted that he's had the opportunity to prove this to others. And his impulse buys reflect his personality; he once almost bought a green fire-engine off eBay!"

With his rugby colleagues he was something of a prankster – though they might have preferred to call him an annoyance. "I was the one messing about, making stupid comments, kneeling behind them so they'd fall over when they stepped back, or putting Deep Heat in Clinchy's jockstrap. I got on like a house on fire with Andy Hobson, which was lucky because he was a big man and I put itching powder in his. On the team bus I liked to sit on the seat behind the steps to the toilet. Once I took a broom handle on so I could lock Anthony Farrell in there; he was a bit claustrophobic. You were together all the time, so you needed to enjoy it, to keep the humour going."

When at Huddersfield, he broke his leg in a pre-season friendly against Leeds, and hobbled around in a pot, unable to train properly. The players went across to a gym near the ground, leaving their valuable locked away and their cars parked outside. "Brandon Costin was also injured and together we got the key to the valuables. We swapped all their bank cards round, then spent about an hour locating all the car keys, and moving their cars to another place. Then we went off for a sandwich. When we got back, a police wagon was there. Paul White was going bonkers because his beloved Golf 1.6 with stripes and stickers had gone missing, and others weren't far behind him. All the keys were in my pocket. I tried to sneak them back, but got busted. There were some angry boys. But they laughed about it afterwards."

He had always been like that. Carl Hall remembers him being just the same at Doncaster. "He wound Tony Fisher up, in a friendly sort of way. And me and Vila Matautia. He was cheeky. Vila would chase after him but could never catch him. Bloemy could run for ever."

At home he is a family man who thinks the world of his wife and kids; he is friendly, easy-going and affable, with a good sense of humour. "He's cheeky and happy-go-lucky," comments wife Louise, "but kind and caring. He puts everybody else in front of himself. He has been amazing when I have been poorly, pulling me through and holding everything together in the home. He's got a soft side to him, he's got a heart." There is always time for the kids – not so much at weekends with his rugby commitments, but at other times. Jordan was brought up on rugby, loved wearing his Halifax kit with "DAD" on the back, and was occasionally a mascot, though he was to grow more into soccer. Isabelle is too young to remember the games, but is aware of what he's done. "She's got his character," says Louise. "She's fiery and confident, a daddy's girl. She's training with Halifax Harriers, so she has sporting genes too."

His mum adds her own praise: "He's got a big heart. He talks big, plays big, everything he does is big. He would help anybody if he could."

Away from home, he is noted for building strong relationships with his customers in his landscaping business. And although he does not often help little old ladies across the road, he does regularly contribute to children's charities, plays Father Christmas at the local school, loves animals, and watches Coronation Street. It is only once he crosses the touchline that Mr Nice becomes Mr Nasty.

At times his on-field persona got him into trouble with the officials. "At the end of the day I have sailed close to the wind for a lot of my career, and when you play the game in that way you have to accept the possible consequences." Yet he was only ever sent off three times in his career. Jim Mills – a Widnes director when Jamie played there, and owner of Legends night club where the players hung out – was dismissed 15 times in British rugby league. Tony Fisher, his coach at Doncaster, Barrie McDermott who he played alongside at Oldham, and Halifax team-mate Paul Davidson, were among many others with far longer disciplinary records.

Even some of the dismissals he feels were questionable. The first, for Doncaster at Oldham, was fair enough, but the others did not result in suspensions. One was at the McAlpine Stadium in Huddersfield when he was playing in an Infirmary Cup match for Halifax, for a supposed spear tackle. It followed a few run-ins with referee Karl Kirkpatrick, with whom he had some history, including a sin-binning earlier in the same match for dissent.

The other was while captaining South Africa in the 2000 World Cup against France. South Africa had lost their first two group games against Papua New Guinea and Tonga, and been heavily penalised. Before the France game he spoke with Australian referee Steve Clark, pointing out the inexperience of many of his team. "I asked him to be lenient, but he didn't appreciate it and said he would officiate how he thought fit. He told me to get lost." After 30 minutes, with South Africa already 14–2 behind, Jamie was sin-binned for interference at a play-the-ball. As he left the field he protested his innocence to coach Paul Matete. Clarke called him back to send him off, thinking Jamie had said something about him. At the judiciary, no further action was taken.

He did have his moments of course. Alan Hadcroft, who joined Halifax at the same time Jamie returned from Huddersfield in 2004, reminded him of their first encounter when Hadcroft was playing for Leigh. Jamie had stood on his hand and broken it. "He said he'd hated me ever since, and I said we'd be fine now and it would have been an accident. He said it wasn't – apparently I'd warned him never to tackle me again." There were a number of sin-binnings along the way, one he remembers being against Rochdale. "I'd tackled the hooker Janan Billings, then lifted him and slammed him on his back. He jumped up and came running, so I smacked him and he fell over. We both got binned even though he hadn't done anything."

He was also placed on report a few times. The first referral was while at Widnes in 1998 when he was found not guilty, and there were three for Halifax – a biting incident with Lee Briers when he was innocent but found guilty, and two when he was not suspended. One was during a pre-season friendly against Castleford in 2001 when he was accused of treading on the head of Adrian Vowles, the other in 2005 for a similar charge when playing against York. On the first occasion he was cleared, the second he was fined.

Many times his aggressive play resulted in his team being penalised, which could annoy the fans and sometimes the coach. While at Doncaster, Tony Fisher left him out for a match for this very reason: "Jamie has been giving away too many penalties in recent games," he told the local press. Yet on occasions he was responding to instructions. He played for lots of different coaches, all with their own views on how they wanted their teams to play. "They were the bosses. If they told me to play a certain way, that's what I'd do. I tried to be a team player rather than do what was best for me. When Halifax were playing Wigan once I was given a roving role to follow Andy Farrell. I was told to wind him up, give him a late shot, or try to engage him in a fight. I gave penalties away for offences I would not normally commit.

"On another occasion against Wigan I was picked at centre to mark Steve Renouf and make sure he did not score. Gavin Clinch told me it would wind him up if I called him Petrol Sniffer, which he said was his nickname back home. In reality Clinchy was setting me up; it was a term that was insulting to someone of Aboriginal descent like Renouf. He got angry and chased after me, hurling blows at my head when I went to make the game's next tackle. Referee Karl Kirkpatrick called him over and warned him, but then sent me to the sin bin. I protested my innocence, but he said Renouf would not have done that unless I had done something first! After the final whistle Renouf came over to say he had enjoyed the game, and we had a beer together.

"In my very last home game for Huddersfield we were playing against Warrington and losing, when a message was brought on by the physio to start a fight. I ran into Nathan Wood the next time I had the ball, got on top of him, and elbowed him as I was getting up. Ben Westwood was there ready to be acting half-back, and he got involved as well, and all three of us got sin-binned. We scored a couple of tries while they were off, so it worked well, though we still lost the game. But I wouldn't have done that without being told to.

"Sometimes we had code words. Playing for Halifax against St Helens, Nick Fozzard was having a great game, running through us. The code word came out that meant I had to create a melee. I gave him a cheap shot. He carried it on and it affected his game. Our supporters got on my back for the penalties, but it was for the good of the team. It's not always what people think. It could help us pick our game up when things were not going well."

Steve Linnane was a coach who favoured a less confrontational approach, changing the way Jamie played. It did not coincide with his greatest games, and for a while he was only on the fringes of first team selection.

Off the field, his unwillingness to stay silent when he felt something needed saying led to fall-outs with some of his coaches, not to mention club officials and referees. Indeed, but for this volatility, he might never have found his way to rugby league, stemming as it did from him telling Western Province officials what he thought of their selection policy.

There was lots more to Jamie's game than aggression of course. It was his strong, fast running out of defence that first brought him praise. A *Yorkshire Post* preview of the Oldham versus Doncaster match in 1994 made the point. "Powerhouse South African full-back Jamie Bloem returns to Watersheddings today having won a host of admirers with his driving runs from defence and powerful finishing near the line." Early press reports of his appearances for Doncaster and Widnes are littered with such references. "A brilliant mid-field break by full-back Jamie Bloem – one of many such runs – carved out the chance," commented Steve Hossack in the *Doncaster Star*, reporting on the Doncaster versus Mysons match in October 1993, Raymond Fletcher reported that "One glorious chance followed a superb break by Jamie Bloem," in the *Yorkshire Post* when Doncaster played Dewsbury, in January 1994. Rick Bolt noted "A barnstorming break out of defence ended 20 yards from the line," in *League Express's* report of Doncaster's clash with Whitehaven in March 1994, and Neil MacDonald said in the *Widnes Weekly News* in July 1997 that "Bloem appeared to be everywhere at once on a day when only one missed conversion and drop kick separated him from a perfect performance."

There was speed – "Bloem raced some sixty yards in a thrilling touchline run," reported Chris Moore in *League Express when* Widnes faced Featherstone in July 1997, and Paul Cook said that Jamie "made the tackle of the match when he turned and chased down Keighley's flying winger Marlon Billy after a 60-yard sprint." [†] And there was kicking – Tom Clarke said that "Bloem's high ball fell favourably for Evans to scurry in at the corner," in *League Express's* report on Doncaster's visit to Barrow in February 1994. Reporting on the Widnes versus Dewsbury match in June 1997, Chris Moore said that "Yet again that man Bloem played a vital role. He launched a towering bomb towards the Rams posts" for Hampson to score. [‡]

After moving into the forwards, it was his workaholic defence and general full-scale effort that won plaudits, allied to his running. "The South African was everywhere in attack and defence as Halifax battled to get their season back on track," wrote James Roberts in the *Halifax Courier*, reporting on Halifax versus London Broncos in May 2000. The same reporter said that "Bloem produced a trademark all-action display, getting through a huge amount of work with and without the ball," when covering Halifax against Salford in the same month. That

---

[†] *Widnes Weekly News*
[‡] *League Express*

season saw him easily top the Halifax tackle count in the Opta Stats, with 726, while he was second behind Darryl Cardiss for tackle busts and second behind Gary Mercer for metres made.

And he was always a goalkicker, though the teams he played for usually had other marksmen as well, meaning he was often the second choice. Oldham had Steve Kerry, Doncaster had Rocky Turner one year and Alex Green the next, while at Huddersfield Steve McNamara kicked most of the goals. Halifax used Martin Pearson in 1998, Graham Holroyd in 1999, and the re-signed Pearson in 2000. For the 2001 season Halifax began with Adam Hughes in the role, but a success rate of six from eleven in the first match persuaded the coaching staff to bring in goalkicking guru Simon Hodgkinson, an England rugby union full-back in the early 1990s. Hodgkinson's view was that young academy star Danny Tickle was the club's most natural kicker, but that Jamie was the more accurate of the first teamers and should take over. "Simon has changed my style a bit," he told the *Halifax Courier*. "I seem to be getting the consistency now." He landed 18 in the next six games, until Tickle's emergence limited his opportunities once more.

Jamie had never previously been coached as a kicker. "Until I was 16 back home we played barefoot, and with the old leather balls. I didn't have the best style, but have always stuck to the same run-up. We didn't have tees, but used sand, as we did in England when I first came over."

Jamie was first choice kicker when he went back to Halifax in 2004, finishing with 91 successes, plus a drop-goal, in his 27 appearances. He kept the job in 2005, but began to be selected more on the bench, so chances were fewer. He still notched 68. "I kicked 11 one game up at Barrow to put me in sight of the club record, but then I got taken off. That was annoying. Someone worked out once that my career average was 73 per cent, not bad for a second choice kicker."

He began his career as a full-back, though regularly featured at wing and centre. For South Africa he became a half-back, before later being more often used in the pack. "I found my feet best in the second row. That was my niche." He was loose-forward a lot at the end of his career, introducing more ball-playing into his game. "I got some moves going with Pat Weisner, who ran off me well and picked up a few tries from me popping the ball up to him." To almost complete a fairly unique set, he had been selected at hooker in Halifax's 47–26 win at Widnes in 2002.

This versatility became his greatest strength; Tony Smith told him once that he was a whole bench rolled into one player. "It gave me longevity," he says. The only position he was never selected in was prop, though he had filled in there in games once or twice. "At the end of my final season I asked Faz to start me there, but he wouldn't let me. I would have liked to have done that, been selected in every position on the field."

His type of game transferred well to rugby union. "Union is a more technical game. Certain league players do well with it, but not forwards. There's a lot less one-on-one." Jamie's upbringing with union in South Africa helped him enormously, but he was generally used as a crash-ball centre in his days with union teams at Widnes and Halifax, plus his county honours with Cheshire and Yorkshire, which has suited several league converts. "I am a second-row in league and a centre in union," he told Sam Wheeler in an interview with the *Yorkshire Post* in 2004. "The roles are the same: batter the ball up the middle." Though the roles were the same, the sports themselves were separate – he never attempted to play-the-ball at Ovenden Park on the Saturday or set up a ruck or maul at The Shay on a Sunday. "I've always enjoyed playing league, but I can enjoy union even more. There is not as much pressure to win. The lads play because they want to, rather than because they are paid to."

At Old Brodleians and Old Rishworthians he was able to use his experience to dictate from the middle of the field, usually from fly-half. Back in rugby league at Stainland it was the same. "I still got sin-binned last week though, and opposition supporters were hurling abuse the week before," he said in late 2011.

3. Where it all began

Rugby came relatively late to Jamie. From a young age he had always been good at sport, but it was karate, tennis and athletics that were to the fore. He represented South Africa at karate, won Springbok colours at tennis, and broke the record at triple jump at Under 16 level. His jump of 15m 62cm still stands as the record seemingly. Long distance running was a forte too, and a little bit of rugby.

He played mostly at full-back and wing, and also had a spell at scrum-half. "But I preferred running out wide and scoring tries," he remembers. "I liked to showboat a bit at that age." The showboating brought an embarrassing moment when he was picked for Craven Week. Named after legendary South African administrator Danie Craven, it was a tournament in which all the best school players were picked for their provincial side to play matches against the other provinces. "There were four of us from the same school in the team, and we put on a move we used in school matches, which ended with me slicing through. I was clear and turned my head round to look for everyone, showing off. When I turned back to put the ball down I hit the post and broke my nose. I still scored because I fell across the line. Snippets from the matches were shown on television, and of course they showed that bit, and I got a lot of ridicule."

He gave up on sport amid the trauma of his dad being killed in the Angolan War in 1986 – Jamie was aged 15 at the time – but took it up again in his last couple of years at school. The school team was a particularly good one, winning the cup competition for all of South Africa. The 1st XV matches attracted huge crowds; the junior teams played earlier and stayed to watch, the opposition sides did too, and lots of others came. "There would be several thousand. It was a big atmosphere. There was a funny moment in one match when one of our forwards tucked the ball up the back of his shirt at a maul and ran off downfield, unnoticed by our opponents." Jamie won provincial colours again, and another trip to Craven Week. "At the end of it they select a Craven XV, and I got in that."

Two years of National Service was a requirement for white, male South Africans between 1967 and 1994. At a loss what to do on leaving school, he took it up straight away, joining the Army in Cape Town. Here the rugby worked to his advantage. Turning out in an inter-base match, he was spotted by the coach for the team that represented the whole of the Defence Force, and was invited to play for them. They were handily based in Cape Town, and made the rest of his army life cushy with regular evening and weekend passes for matches. The sports involvement also played a minor part in helping him negotiate an honourable early discharge, though not before a stressful stint on the front line.

A friend played for the Milnerton club, so he joined them, playing first for the under–21s, then progressing to the seniors, at wing, centre, or full-back. He soon made a mark, and won press recognition for the first time. In a home defeat against Goodwood at Newlands, *The Argus* said that "On the wing, Jamie Bloem was the only backline player to shine for Milnerton." He took over the goalkicking; in one match against Belhar he nailed six conversions and a penalty to add to a try. His career took off and he won selection for the Western Province under–20s regional side, stopping the athletics and other sports to give it his full attention. "I represented Western Province for two seasons from the age of 19, playing alongside four future Springboks, including Danie Gerber. My debut was in front of 75,000 people."

Now he could start to be ambitious. "All young players in South Africa dream of playing for the Springboks, but the competition is immense." Another try and six goals performance, this time for Western Province early in the 1992–93 season, left him on a high, only for him to be dropped the following week when Springbok full-back Mike Bayly returned from injury. Always being one to stand up for himself, he argued the point and ended up falling out.

It just so happened that his last match had been watched by Tony Lane, a former Lock Lane amateur rugby league player originally from Castleford, who told him his aggressive style of play would be more suited to rugby league. There had been some rugby league played in South Africa in the early 1960s, and fresh attempts to get it going at an amateur level in recent years, but Jamie had never even heard of the game. He watched the Australian and English match videos that Tony lent him however, and liked what he saw.

A few South African amateur rugby league teams now existed, including one in Cape Town where Jamie lived, playing occasional games. Because of the vast size of South Africa, arranging fixtures was problematical, so they tended to play in tournaments, with all teams coming together in one area over a weekend. One such tournament had been held in Pretoria in early 1992, sponsorship from Magnis Nissan making it possible. Cape Town Coasters were unable to make an impression, but tournament winners Durban and Pretoria Bulls fielded a few top provincial players, and the standard was quite good.

Another tournament was fixed for October 1992, sponsored this time by a stockbroking firm, Boner and Freemantle Inc. Jamie was easily persuaded by Tony Lane to have a go with Cape Town Coasters. They had to travel 1000 miles to Megawatt Park in Johannesburg to take part, but thrashed the local side Johannesburg Nomads 40–6 in the first match. "Eventually on the Saturday evening the final was played between the tremendously fit and motivated Cape Town side and Pretoria Bulls, the top Transvaal side," reported *South African Rugby League,* a magazine issued by that organisation itself, the SARFL. "The game was an incredible spectacle of open rugby with the fitness of the Cape Town side proving too much for the gallant Pretoria team." They won by 38–6; among the interested spectators being Widnes chairman Jim Mills and Halifax director Robert Atkinson.

Supposedly by 1992 a free gangway for amateur players existed between union and league all over the world, but the league players received plenty of flak in South Africa. After the final whistle the victors gathered for drinks and to dance to Tina Turner's *Simply the Best* blaring from the PA system, but "through it all, there was the underlying threat from mighty rugby union", wrote one newspaper. "Most weren't too worried, and at least two players shouted out: 'Rugby union can go to hell!' Most were disillusioned with rugby union and a group of coloured[§] supporters on the sidelines were vociferous in their condemnation of what they saw as white-dominated SARFU and the lip service paid to rugby development."

Scheduled for November were two test matches, the first international rugby league fixtures to be played in South Africa since the 1960s. They were to be against the visiting Russian national side, also relative newcomers to the international scene. Rugby league had developed there in the late 1980s. The national side, the Russian Bears, had been formed in 1991 to meet the touring English teams York and Fulham, and played France for the first time the same year.

[§] In South Africa under apartheid, 'coloured' was used to classify people of mixed race.

Jamie had heard about these forthcoming internationals, and harboured hopes that he had done enough to impress the selectors, so was delighted to be told that he had been picked for the team, to be known as the South African Rhinos. His new sport was working well for him. Indeed rugby league looked to have a great future in South Africa. It appealed to the coloured communities and attracted a lot of interest. "There were seven coloured boys in the Cape Town Coasters, and six in the international selection," remembers Jamie.

This growth in league did not impress the union authorities. "The South African Rugby Football Union will ban any player who plays amateur rugby league in South Africa," wrote Mark Keohane in the *Cape Times*. "The latest move in the league-union rivalry came yesterday when star Natal centre Dick Muir informed SARFU of his intention to play for the South African rugby league national team, the Rhinos, in Friday night's first test against the Russians in Johannesburg."

SARFU argued that the agreement on the free gangway between the codes was at the discretion of each national executive. General manager Arrie Oberholzer announced that they decided against it "because it allows amateur league to get a foothold and ultimately the scenario is the amateur league game turns professional. We don't impede the rights of the individual and they are free to play either league or union. They cannot play both."

Dick Muir clearly had an interest in rugby league, for he had played a couple of secret trials with Halifax second team the previous March. One was a Friday night at Thrum Hall, when a crowd of 1,499 saw him kick two goals in a 38–18 victory over St Helens, but terms could not be agreed. The SARFU pronouncements persuaded him to withdraw from the international – he later won five rugby union caps with South Africa - but the squad did include "several promising Western Province club players," reported Keohane, "most notably Milnerton and Western Province under–21 fullback Jamie Bloem,"

The Russians, fresh from a 28–6 loss to France in Toulouse, flew into South Africa less than 12 hours before kick-off for the match on Friday 13 November 1992 at Milner Park, Johannesburg. South African journalist Clinton van der Berg recorded that "a top-class Rhinos team turned out and opened the scoring with a try by right centre John Assor." By half-time, however, the Russians were in front 14–10, and went on to edge out the South Africans 30–26. Jamie converted three of his team's six tries in the wet and windy conditions. "Capetonian and former Milnerton fullback Jamie Bloem impressed for the national team in the last line of defence," wrote Mark Keohane, though the match had ended disappointingly for him. Clinton van der Berg finished his match report by saying "the writing was on the wall when a Russian dropkick attempt fell short, only to have Bloem knock on into opposing full-back Dimitriy Schlimmer's hands, finding the try-line barely a few metres away." The attendance was recorded as 2,000.

The second test was played seven days later, this time at Berea Park in Pretoria. Jamie was again on the losing side as the Russians won 22–19 in front of 3,000 spectators. The Rhinos had made a couple of team changes, "but Russia were all fired up and had clearly attuned themselves to altitude and playing conditions," observed van der Berg. "A vociferous home crowd were rewarded when tempestuous Jamie Bloem put over a drop from 20m out," and he later added three more conversions.

"Once I started playing league," says Jamie, "I realised how much more it has to offer. You have to attack the ball at pace when you are taking it and not stand around waiting for it like you do in union." And it had now made him into an international rugby player.

Jamie with his wife Louise and Paul Myler at Widnes.
(Photo: Aaron Photographers)

Jamie and Louise with Jordan and Isabelle at the Galpharm (now John Smith)
Stadium in Huddersfield in 2009.

28

FIRST RUGBY LEAGUE INTERNATIONAL
TOUR IN SOUTH AFRICA

'BEWARE THE BEAR'

SOUTH AFRICAN RHINOS versus RUSSIAN BEARS

1st Test
13 November 1992
Wits Stadium, Jhb
17h00

2nd Test
20 November 1992
Berea Park, Pretoria
17h00

Sponsored by

 **MARVOL**

 HELIOS POWER **CONCORDE TRAVEL**

 R5.00 SOUVERNIR PROGRAMME

South Africa versus Russia programme cover –
Jamie's international debut in November 1992.

Cape Town Coasters, Jamie's first rugby league team. Jamie is in the back row, fourth right.

South Africa versus Russia in 1992. Jamie is in the back row, fourth left.

4. Castleford

Jamie had taken to amateur rugby league, but it rapidly became the professional game that was in his sights now that he knew about it. The chance to be part of what he had seen on Tony Lane's videos was vastly appealing. Not that he could have gone back to union anyway. "I received a fax informing me I was banned from the union game in South Africa," he says. "It was made clear that I would never play for Western Province again, and that I had surrendered any ambition I might have had of playing for South Africa 'B' or any other representative side."

To play professionally would mean moving abroad to either England or Australia. Rhinos team-mate Jacob Steemag took up an offer of trials with Australian outfit Penrith Panthers, but for Jamie it was England that beckoned. Several South Africans had followed that route earlier, including Mike Brown to Halifax in 1962, and his mother was already living there, having moved to Stockton-On-Tees near Middlesbrough two years after his dad died, along with his brother and sisters. More significantly, Tony Lane had contacts in England, and was able to fix him up with a trial at Castleford. The Wheldon Road outfit paid for his flight. It helped that he would not count on the club's overseas register, coming as he did from a "developing" rugby league nation, and with a British passport to boot.

By this time Jamie had a wife Leigh and three-month old son Tevern in Cape Town, but within just a few days of the second test, he was on his way. Leigh chose not to go with him. "Milnerton rugby star Jamie Bloem is going to try his luck in the professional ranks of rugby league in Britain," wrote Lester Mills in the *Northern Argus* on 25 November. "He is quietly confident he can make it in a league where more seasoned South African campaigners like Tom Van Vollenhoven, Ray Mordt and Rob Louw became household names."

"I was young and impulsive," remembers Jamie, but it was the best thing he could have done and he has never looked back. After arriving at Manchester Airport, it was off through what seemed a sea of orange lights in the dark, to Castleford. Home for a while was to be the Wheldale Hotel (now called The Boot Room), owned by Brian and Mavis, who were like a mum and dad to him.

Castleford were a decent side. In the previous season they had finished third in the Stones Bitter Championship behind Wigan and St Helens, had won the Yorkshire Cup, and had reached the Challenge Cup Final at Wembley, where they had lost 28–12 to Wigan, in May. Their successful coach was Darryl van der Velde, an Australian who as a player had represented his state Queensland in 1977, and had been at Castleford since 1988.

"He proved to be a good coach," says Jamie. "I learned a lot from him; rugby league is difficult to master when you are new to it. He gave me a chance and always looked after me, though I felt that he didn't stick to all the original promises. I have a lot of respect for him."

The deal with Castleford was to play initially in the seconds, the Alliance team, on £200 per week. That was duly forthcoming the first week, but the second he was presented with just £50. "That's what Darryl has told me to give you," explained the secretary.

One of the players was Tawera Nikau, the New Zealand international, who went with him to buy new boots. Jamie was looking at the cheaper pairs, but Tawera called him across to the top-of-the-range section. "What are you looking at those for?" he asked, so Jamie explained about the £50 wages. That evening, he was visited by Tawera's wife, Letitia. Mrs Nikau was a formidable lady, who acted as her husband's agent. "Show me your contract," she said. Jamie explained that he didn't have one. She led him across the road to the ground, where a proper agreement was signed and Jamie was back to £200 a week.

Richie Blackmore, Nikau's fellow Kiwi star, was also at Castleford. Between the pair they came up with "Bushpig" as a nickname for him. "I think it was the only South African creature they knew of," suggests Jamie in explanation. Apparently it can be quite aggressive though, so there might have been some thought involved. Regardless, the name did not survive long after leaving Castleford, and he soon became simply "Bloemy".

Like a young football apprentice, he was given the job of cleaning boots. "It was like an initiation thing. Blackmore's were size 13!"

He made his first appearance for the Wheldon Road club in the second team at Bradford on Friday 27 November, just a few days after arriving in the country, scoring a try in a 26–14 victory. He remembers the shirt as much as anything, with pads on the shoulders. "It felt like a duvet," he says. "I was a winger!" The following week the seniors were at home to Second Division outfit Carlisle in the second round of the Regal Trophy. It was the perfect opportunity to give him a run, and he was duly selected to make his first team debut from the substitute's bench on Sunday 6 December.

Full-back Graham Steadman was missing, but Castleford fielded a formidable team: Simon Middleton, St John Ellis, Richie Blackmore, Tony Smith, Jon Wray, Peter Coyne, Mike Ford, Lee Crooks, Chris Watson, Dean Sampson, Tony Morrison, Martin Ketteridge, Tawera Nikau. Subs: Jamie Bloem, Keith England.

He went on after half-time in place of Jon Wray on the wing, with Castleford already leading 28–0. There was plenty of time to make an impact though, which he did with a try late on. "Ford and Blackmore gave Bloem the chance to show his finishing ability," reported the *Yorkshire Post*, for "one of the best tries of the game." Nigel Brookes wrote in *The Yorkshire Evening Post* that "stand-in winger, South African Jamie Bloem, had an interesting first-team debut. He had very little chance to shine with the ball but did his best to make up for it by tackling everything that moved on the left flank."

"Castleford's South African trialist Jamie Bloem made an impressive debut in yesterday's Regal Trophy clash at Wheldon Road," recorded the *Yorkshire Post* in a separate article, "scoring a try in the First Division side's 54–0 thrashing of Carlisle." It was enough to win him a place *in League Express's* "Team of the Week" on the Monday morning.

Reports even reached South Africa, where *The Argus* correspondent Mark Keohane told readers that "Jamie Bloem's rugby league career got off to the fairy tale start that eluded such greats as former All Black full-back John Gallagher." He quoted an elated Jamie as saying, "It was great to be a part of a first team game, and to score a try was a bonus. I was fortunate that the opposition were overrun by Castleford, so the only pressure was on myself when I came on. Had the opposition been stronger and Castleford struggling it could have been a little different. My real test is still to come."

His coach was somewhat non-committal. "I have got a couple more weeks to make a decision about him," said Van der Velde. "He has got some flaws in his game which will have to be rectified, but he has not played a lot of rugby league."

Scoring a try for Castleford 'A' against Featherstone Rovers in 1992.

Castleford's next match was against high-flying St Helens. "Newcomer Jamie Bloem is set to lose his place on the bench," announced John Callaghan in the *Yorkshire Post*. Van der Velde was reported as saying, "He did very well and that was just the right sort of game in which to introduce him. He has a lot to learn though, and St Helens are a very different proposition altogether."

He played another 'A' (second) team game, but things were not working out as he would have liked. The contract problems and doubts that he could cement a regular first team place at Castleford unsettled him and led to thoughts of returning home. "Everyone at Castleford made me very welcome, but I was realistic enough to know that, at that early stage of my rugby league involvement, I was not in their league. Castleford were a top club chasing honours, and I don't think they really had the time to spend on showing me all I needed to know." They had 25 full-time professionals and only two part-timers. Graham Steadman was established at full-back, Simon Middleton and St John Ellis on the wings.

In his absence the first team won their championship match against St Helens, then beat the same opposition at Knowsley Road in the next round of the Regal Trophy, before losing at Bradford in the semi-final.

34

5. Oldham

A better option for Jamie would be to have another go at a lower level. Darryl van der Velde contacted Aussie mate Peter Tunks, who was coaching at Oldham, and Jamie agreed to play there, while continuing to live at the Wheldale Hotel in Castleford. Oldham were a second division side (there were three divisions at this time), but riding high and challenging strongly for promotion. Still at Watersheddings, they were a good club to join. "I am sure I will be better off in the Second Division," Jamie told *Oldham Evening Chronicle* journalist Roger Halstead. "I suppose my future will depend on how I shape up over the next few weeks."

Letitia Nikau helped him sort out a contract, though his potential debut against Bramley on Sunday 20 December ended up succumbing to the weather. The Swinton match at Gigg Lane went the same way, leaving no action until the New Year. Two games in four days, both against Bramley and both at Watersheddings, part of an odd fixture list that required teams to meet four times in a season, finally presented the opportunity.

Against a Bramley side featuring future playing colleague Sonny Whakarau, Jamie's first Oldham appearance came on Wednesday 6 January. The team was: Wally Gibson, Jamie Bloem, Gary Christie, Iva Ropati, Scott Ranson, Tommy Martyn, Steve Kerry, Ian Sherratt, Richard Russell, Mark Sheals, Shane Tupaea, David Bradbury, Richard Pachniuk. Subs: Steve Warburton and Joe Graziano. He did not score in a 36–0 victory, but in the Sunday match he powered over for a try in the corner in a similarly emphatic 40–2 success.

The season continued successfully, Oldham coasting to promotion in second place behind Featherstone Rovers, 11 points clear of third-placed Huddersfield. An agreement had quickly been reached to stay with Oldham for the rest of the season and potentially the following season too. "It's a good club," he told the local press. "I am happy at Oldham and I wouldn't mind committing myself to five or six years."

He had made a good impression. "He was raw at first," remembered Roger Halstead in 2012, "but strong, pacy and absolutely fearless, the sort of player who excited the crowd because they sensed he was capable of doing something out of the ordinary." He made his mark off the field too. "He was a very forthright young man," added Halstead, "confident, determined to do well and keen to make an impact."

Jamie made 11 full appearances plus one from the bench in that 1992–93 season, all of them on the wing apart from one appearance at full-back at Carlisle on 17 January. It could have been more – and it certainly could have been less – following a horrific injury suffered in the third round of the Challenge Cup.

Having beaten London Crusaders and Huddersfield in earlier rounds, Jamie registering his second Oldham try in the Huddersfield tie on Valentine's Day, the club were again drawn at home on 3 March. The opponents this time were the much more formidable Bradford Northern, then riding high in third place in the top division, the Stones Bitter Championship, with a team featuring Brian Noble, David Hobbs, Karl Fairbank, Roy Powell and Tony Anderson among others. Bradford eventually won 42–4, but by then Jamie was in hospital. A tackle by former Leeds and Halifax international forward Paul Medley had left him with a suspected broken neck.

"There was nothing wrong with the tackle," says Jamie. "I didn't see Paul coming from the side because I was concentrating on Steve McGowan in front of me. Paul hit me with a shoulder charge, knocked me down, and then fell on top of me. My head was pushed forward between my legs and it was that which caused the problems."

He lost all feeling below the neck, so clearly it was serious. Oldham physiotherapist Nick Hodgson was joined by doctors from both clubs, who fitted a surgical collar before lifting him on to a stretcher, the game being held up for several minutes. With it being a cup tie, an ambulance was on stand-by. "We might have had a problem had it been a Second Division match," the club doctor told the *Oldham Evening Chronicle*, "because the ambulance would not have been there." The recent Taylor Report had demanded that ambulances be stationed at sports events attracting crowds of more than 5,000. The actual attendance was 5,405.

Early suggestions in Royal Oldham Hospital were that he might not play rugby again, or even walk, as there was still no feeling. He was fitted with a cage, and the nurses had to keep turning him every so often. But soon afterwards, as he was being given a bed-bath, he suddenly started to feel an irritation from the brush being used. The nurse rushed off to fetch the doctors, whose tests showed that his feeling was indeed returning. Their tests and x-rays proved that their initial fears were unfounded. He had suffered no fractures or dislodged bones, rather badly torn and wrenched ligaments and muscles in his back and neck. The medical view now was that he would be out for the season, but thereafter fine to return.

He awoke the following day to find an unknown lady at his bedside. "Hi," she said.

"I'm sorry," Jamie replied. "I don't know who you are."

"I'm Paul Medley's mum," she continued, though he still didn't understand until she explained that Paul had been involved in the tackle where he got hurt. She had heard he had no family in the country, and moved over from Bradford to a hotel in Oldham to be with him until he left hospital, reading to him from newspapers and magazines. "It was awesome," recalls Jamie. We still text each other, and I still see Paul regularly, like when I referee at Bradford.

Well-wishers sent their best regards. A card from "Louise – age 9 – Hutchins Stand" said "Hurry up and get back in that No. 2 shirt". And Stuart Broadbent wrote a letter from Leeds to the Oldham club: "As a supporter of rugby league, both me and my family hope that Jamie is not too badly injured, and that he may be able to resume playing very soon."

After 48 hours he was able to be released from hospital to move in temporarily with his mum in the North-East. His back remained painful, but full movement was returning to his neck. Wife Leigh flew in from Cape Town with son Tevern, suggesting he return with them, but that was not what he wanted to do, and after a few days they left. Within three weeks he was back training with Oldham, and returning to action with the second team. "I have healed quickly," he told the *Oldham Chronicle.* "I'm defying the doctors, but I feel marvellous."

Roger Halstead reported no ill-effects. "Considering the extent of his injuries and the speed of his recovery, Bloem produced a splendid performance at full-back," he wrote. Another impressive display in the next match, coupled with the first team's shock defeat at home to London Crusaders, brought a return to senior duty in the rematch at Crystal Palace on 31 March. Also back from injury that day was young prop forward Barrie McDermott, who had seen a lot of Jamie's play. In his autobiography he wrote that Jamie was a "winger who can give front-rowers a tough time." He was, added McDermott, "the sort of bloke who could get into a fight with his own shadow."

A highlight of the remaining matches was a 28–24 home victory over Huddersfield on Easter Monday, achieved in great adversity. Before half-time Oldham had lost three players with match-ending injuries, and had Barrie McDermott sent off for a high tackle on Gary Coulter. With only two substitutes in those days, there were 45 minutes to play with 11 players, and Huddersfield 12–0 ahead by the interval. "Those 11 men rolled up their sleeves and did a truly magnificent job," wrote Roger Halstead in the *Chronicle*. "It was Rorke's Drift all over again; 11 men against 13 and a glorious victory to the 11." It suited Jamie's game to a tee, and he was well to the fore.

The end-of-season play-offs should have been another highlight. Under the system of the time, promotion was already achieved, the play-offs being a separate competition, but an opportunity both for medals and the chance to play at Old Trafford in the final. Jamie, though, was not in the team, a row with coach Peter Tunks seeing him sidelined. Oldham crashed out after drawing 14–14 at home to Dewsbury in the first game, and losing the replay 20–18.

"I said later in the press that I regretted signing for Oldham, but it was not the club that was a regret, just the coach. He persuaded me to go there, but then didn't stick to the promises. The contract, more or less the same money as at Castleford and a continuation of the accommodation payments there, seemed fine. Later they got me a terraced house in Oldham so that the family could visit again, but then they stopped paying the rent. My wages suddenly reduced as well and I couldn't afford to keep the house on. I almost decided to go home with Leigh and Tevern. Luckily Iva Ropati, one of the overseas players, heard about it and said I could move in with him. Iva's a nice guy. He didn't have to do that. I stayed with him for the rest of the season."

Peter Tunks suggested that if he wasn't happy he should find another club, but he was still new to the country and had no contacts. Letitia Nikau had done well for him, so he decided to acquire an agent, signing up with Derek Parker. Continuing with Oldham was still an option, as he had enjoyed playing for them and got on well with the fans and his team-mates. With promotion though, Oldham would be in the top division in 1993–94, Parker's advice being that it would be preferable to stay in the lower division and get to know the game better. A good deal was available from ambitious Doncaster, a Third Division side in 1992–3 but seemingly with money to throw around under chairman John Desmond. And further, they presented the opportunity to turn out at full-back rather than on the wing, where he had been utilised at Oldham and Castleford. Jamie signed for them for a year, with the option of an additional year afterwards.

Coach Tony Fisher announced the news to the media. "Jamie is determined to do well," he said. "The contract will be based on incentives. He will have to do well to fulfil it, but I was impressed with his keenness."

Some were sad to see him leave. Oldham fan Christine Wilcox wrote him a letter: "This is just a note to say how sorry myself, my family and many Oldham fans are not to see you in Oldham colours next year. Your attacking play, your ability to take up the ball and help the forwards, and your great courage to return to play after your injury in the Bradford match, soon made you a favourite with the fans."

That was nice, and he has kept the letter. But it was time to move on. His career in rugby league was about to take off.

Playing for Doncaster against Featherstone, 1993–94.

Civic reception for the Doncaster side that won promotion in 1994.
Jamie is to the right of the mayor.

6. Doncaster

Joining Doncaster in 1993 brought Jamie the craziest 18 months of his life. The team had finished seventh in Division Three in the previous 1992–93 season, but the leagues had been restructured into just two divisions, meaning even tougher fixtures in the campaign ahead. The Dons meant to meet the challenge full on. They had also signed New Zealander Sonny Whakarau, fellow-Kiwi Carl Hall was back for another stint at the club, and a third, Vila Matautia, was soon to follow – plus Andy Clarke had joined from Castleford, and Rocky Turner from Warrington for £15,000. Aussie Brad Hayes also returned for a second season. "I was taken by what the club were doing. They were building a good team." The story goes that director of football John Sheridan was so impressed with the summer signings that he laid £10 on them at odds of 100–1 to win promotion.

For much of their history, Doncaster had been near the bottom of the entire league, often in last place. But in 1986 local businessman and likeable Irishman John Desmond had come to the club's aid, loaning money to bring about a revival. Tony Fisher, the former Wales and Great Britain hooker, had become coach in November 1992 after spells at Bramley and Keighley, and set about building a stronger, and more expensive, team than the club had experienced before.

Fisher, known as one of the game's hard men as a player, continued his style as a coach, being aggressive and demanding. He was supportive of his player though, and able to motivate them to perform at their best. "He was an old school type coach," remembers Jamie. "He had us running through tyres, carrying tyres, going on hikes with bags of sand on our backs, that sort of thing. Nothing like today. We'd play touch and pass after training, while he stood in the middle with his arms folded, but if anyone ran near him he'd stick out an arm and send them crashing to the floor. Yet it all seemed to work. We were so close as a group."

As part of pre-season training he took the players away together, not to Lanzarote or America, but to Skipton. "The bus stopped by a farmer's field, full of sheep. He told us we all had to bring him a sheep, and we wouldn't be leaving until we had all done so. It was quite late before everyone had succeeded. Then he announced that what we should have done was use teamwork – worked together. He'd never said that earlier, we didn't know it was allowed.

"We stayed in a hostel, with a couple of young women thrown in. It was all quite bizarre. I wondered what I was coming to! But we all got on so well. It became a bit like the Crazy Gang at Wimbledon Football Club during the 1980s and 1990s. We were a team of misfits really – one of them had a criminal record. We weren't the most gifted of teams, just a crazy bunch of people who had a great time."

The set-up at Tattersfield was good, but unlike anywhere Jamie had played before or since. "The changing rooms were two Portacabins, not even close together. And once, the club mistakenly ordered 120 tons of sea sand instead of the proper stuff for the grass. So the grass didn't grow and we all ended up with cut knees. Tony Fisher liked to upset the opposition, so he'd hide rotting fish in their Portacabin or wire up the tannoy system to blare loud music in there. The club was run so wrongly, but at the same time so right!"

Although most of his team-mates were part-timers, Jamie and the other leading players were full-time professionals. Part of his job was to work on the club lottery and commercial side. "There were six of us – Clarke, Turner, Whakarau, Hall, Matautia and me." His other role was with South Yorkshire development officers John Kear and Ralph Rimmer, visiting schools in Doncaster and Sheffield and working with the kids. It was an enjoyable lifestyle, and in time the pay became very good. The club provided him with a bungalow at Ackworth, where Whakarau came to stay until they found him accommodation of his own. Leigh and Tevern flew over again, and Whakarau's wife arrived as well. Ackworth was quite a drive away, nearer Wakefield than Doncaster, so Jamie moved to another bungalow nearer the ground.

Leigh, however, soon became homesick. "The relationship wasn't going anywhere. We had been forced together through circumstances. She was never happy in Doncaster, didn't like rugby, and would have struggled to fit in. I knew that would be it when she went back to South Africa, and she divorced me. She has gone on to better herself, like I have, so it was the best thing."

Later house guests were the two Pierres, South Africans who played trials for the Dons in 1994. Pierre Assor had been in the squad with Jamie at the 1993 World Sevens, while Pierre Grobbelaar was to become part of the 1995 World Cup selection until a positive test for anabolic steroid Nandrolone saw him banned. "I took them on a visit to a sponsor, where Assor worked his way through a bowl of fruit on the table. We nicknamed him 'Fruit Bat'." Neither player was retained.

Carl Hall, who since 2009 has been Doncaster's chief executive and owner, remembers that Jamie was smaller then, with a stronger South African accent that could be hard to understand. "He was my weight training partner. He was only about 12 stones then, but became stronger than me. He was special, but a moody bugger. We had some good times together. We went on a run once, Audley and Sonny were there too, and ended up at Audley's house. He had some shears, and we decided to all shave our heads. Jamie had some nice long hair then, but was always up for anything and went first. We thought about not following, but then we all got sheared."

On the field, the season developed into a great one. The first match was a pre-season visit to Owlerton to play First Division Sheffield for the Jewson's South Yorkshire Cup. The Eagles, seeking a fourth successive victory in the competition, were firm favourites to most, but the Dons players had an air of confidence and won 20–6. Though of relatively minor importance, it was their first trophy success in their 40-year history. Steve Hossack, in the *Doncaster Free Press*, wrote that "Jamie Bloem hardly put a foot wrong on his debut", while Tony Fisher was also full of praise. "I thought our man-of-the-match, Jamie Bloem, was outstanding," he said. The Doncaster team was: Steve Robson, Audley Pennant, Jamie Bloem, Carl Hall, Mark Roache, Tony Zelei, Alex Green, Andy Clarke, Andy Gascoigne, Ian Fletcher, Sonny Whakarau, Neil Battye, Brad Hayes. Subs: Rob Turner, Tony Miller, Martin Rowse, Tony Bowes, Mark Youngs.

The official odds on winning the title had fallen to 66–1 against, still well out of line with how the team was progressing. "The bookies don't know the score," commented Tony Fisher at the time. "I hope we make them regret being so generous."

He was to almost get his wish, his team eventually finishing just one league point behind champions Workington Town. And the season nearly ended where it had begun, with a trophy. Dewsbury were swamped 48–18 in the Premiership play-offs, to bring a bumper crowd of 3,238 to Tattersfield for the semi-final against London Crusaders, only for the visitors to beat them 16–6.

43

The league season had started in the plush surroundings of Elland Road, with a 32–28 success against its residents at the time, Hunslet, where praises for Jamie continued. "The stand-out figure in Doncaster's second successive win at Elland Road was their South African full-back Jamie Bloem. He looks a player who will make Castleford and Oldham regret not having a longer look at him. Bloem made just one error – and it cost his side a try – but everything else he did had the hallmark of class. The Dons can't believe they managed to pick up such a class player so cheaply."

He starred again in the following week's victory over Bramley. John Anderson in the *Rugby Leaguer* recorded that "Man-of-the-match Jamie Bloem was starting to give Bramley a hard time with his running from deep and safe handling and deserved his try in the corner after 28 minutes." It was his first of eight scores in what were to be 34 appearances that season, plus four goals in the two matches regular marksman Rocky Turner was out injured. The first of the goals came in a 20–0 victory over Oldham in the fifth round of the Challenge Cup the following February. Dons assistant coach Ian Brooke, the former Wakefield Trinity star, paid tribute to his stand-in kicker for landing a vital 40-yard penalty: "What a time to kick your first goal for a club," he said to the press.

There were a few defeats after the promising start, but a run of seven consecutive league wins in mid-winter set them up nicely. One was a stunning 34–18 triumph on New Years' Day against leaders Huddersfield in their temporary residence at Huddersfield Town's Leeds Road. Steve Hossack wrote that Jamie "showed just why he is rated one of the most exciting No 1's outside the top flight when making the running for two of the Dons' six tries," and he was chosen as man-of-the-match in *League Express*.

"The game plan was usually fairly basic," says Jamie. "Five drives and a kick, waiting for the opposition to make a mistake. We would often play with three props in the front row, with one ball-player feeding their runs, and us backs seeing little of the ball." Yet the back section included Carl Hall, Mark Roache, Jamie himself and his best mate Audley Pennant. "One match at Tattersfield we were 18–2 down at half-time. Back in the changing rooms Audley and I stood up and said we thought we should get the ball to the backs. Tony Fisher took us outside behind the Portacabin and drew a line with his toe in the soil. 'If you're man enough," he challenged, 'step over that line!' We weren't interested in fighting him though, so he ordered us back inside. 'These two think they can coach better than me,' he announced, 'so they're in charge now.' And he walked out. None of us had much idea what to do, but we agreed to throw the ball about more and ended up winning. As we left the field, Audley and I decided we'd better apologise to Tony, but as we arrived back he met us with, 'There, I told you we could do it,' and it was never mentioned again. In some ways I thought that Tony Fisher was a disturbed man, but in his own way he was very good. I've got to give him big praise. I still text him."

In addition to the good form in the league, there was also a decent run in the Challenge Cup. Victory over Wigan St Patrick's, Dewsbury and Oldham put the Dons into the quarter finals for only the third time in their history. Drawn away to St Helens they eventually crashed out 40–9, but the scoreline did scant justice to a battling performance. Jamie won praise in the *Doncaster Star* for one "magnificent 40-yard run", but brickbats for a sin-binning. "Not for the first time, Bloem's temper got the better of him after being tackled by Paul Loughlin, and he was shown the yellow card for throwing a punch."

Brian McDermott arrived for a few games on loan from Bradford Northern, and scored a hat-trick against Carlisle. There was another long run of success towards the end of the season, eight in a row this time. Among them was a club-record 96–0 thrashing of Highfield. Jamie's second try was the one that set the record. It was a spectacular 50-metre effort that helped make him man-of-the-match in the *Rugby Leaguer*. With promotion to the top flight determined by league placings, the wins set up a crucial final match of the league season at Batley with a win needed by both teams for the second promotion place.

Crowds had been building, from around 1,000 at the start of the season, to twice that by the end. There were 1,946 for a home win over table-topping Workington Town in February, 4,208 against Huddersfield and 2,723 against Dewsbury in April. For the decider at Batley on 24 April there were 4,500. A tense match was locked at 0–0 for long enough, but two late Doncaster tries saw them win 10–5. A great moment for the Dons, whose followers surged on to the pitch to carry their heroes back to the changing rooms, then stayed behind to celebrate with them and their coach, hero Tony Fisher.

But it all came at a cost. Fisher made sure his stars were well paid. Jamie had started on around £100 a week, plus a similar additional amount for a win, but once he had proved his worth it escalated. "With house and car, I ended up on the equivalent of £1,500 a week," says Jamie, "so the other full-timers will have been getting the same. Some of it was through sponsorship, but John Desmond used to bring the cash portion in envelopes in a suitcase on a Friday." It was an incredible amount of money, more than he was to earn later in Super League, but it was what he was offered rather than what he asked for. "I didn't use it wisely. I should have put half of it away, but I wasted it. Lots of visits to restaurants, gambling on the horses and so on."

Eventually, some of it was spent on Louise. Doncaster did some of their training at The Dome Leisure Centre, where the players had passes for the gym and pool. Louise worked there in the marketing department, usually office-based. One day in the summer of 1994 she was working front of house, handing out leaflets, wearing a uniform with name badge. "Jamie approached and asked my name," remembers Louise. "I thought he was a wide boy, messing around. I had a boyfriend at the time, but we became friends. I split with my boyfriend in October, and we started going out soon afterwards. He'd been married before, and we said we wouldn't be in each other's pockets, but we ended up seeing each other every night because we got on. We still feel like that, we don't get bored with each other. I hadn't been a rugby league fan, but I started going to the matches."

Despite the increased crowds the team enjoyed in their promotion season, the money that had spent on players took its toll. It was all too much for them, cracks had appeared early on, and by the season's end a financial crisis loomed. Debts of nearly £1million were revealed, a winding-up order being narrowly avoided in July. Good though the season was, it had been punctuated with the release of players and threats of wage cuts; at one point the club said they were willing to listen to offers for Jamie and others. Ian Proctor reported in the *Rugby Leaguer* that John Desmond had pumped in a fortune, but that his company had decided enough was enough.

Thoughts of top-flight rugby and big gates against the top clubs provided hope that things would get better. But work needed doing on the ground, and more new players were required. There would clearly be problems ahead. And even more serious ones for Jamie himself.

7. Lifeline at Widnes

The 1994–95 season began with Doncaster topping the entire rugby league pyramid, but soon turned to despair for both Jamie and the club. His drugs ban ended his involvement, and coincided with a losing run by the team. Only one more match was won, and one drawn, leaving them bottom of the table by some distance. Worse still, the financial situation had deteriorated further, the ground was sold, and the majority of the players eventually dispersed to other clubs. While Jamie had initially flirted with giving up the game, his plan quickly became to get back into rugby league when the ban ended.

In his absence the game had changed dramatically. Rupert Murdoch's News Corporation had paid £87 million for a five-year deal to form Super League, the chosen teams gaining a huge influx of cash. While the plan at first had been for mergers, that had been jettisoned in the face of huge opposition from supporters, but the move to summer for professional rugby league had become a reality. Developments around the same time in rugby union were also significant. The former amateur game became 'open' and allowed professional players for the first time; it meant for one thing that league players could join union clubs for the off-season, as many did.

Jamie had set himself a target of reaching the new Super League – effectively his level when playing at Doncaster – and winning international honours again. "A few coaches had announced that they would never sign me, and I knew there were a few people who didn't think I should be allowed back. Even today there are those who believe I should not be allowed to referee. I did wrong, I know that, but I felt I'd accepted my punishment and it was now time to move on."

Returning to Doncaster was a possibility. Tony Fisher had said that he would leave the door open for him. "Jamie knows he has done wrong," he had told the *Rugby Leaguer* at the time of the suspension. "No purpose would be served by punishing him further when he has served his time." Fisher had left Doncaster soon after Jamie though. The club had reformed as Doncaster Dragons, playing in the lowest division at Meadow Court Greyhound Stadium in Stainforth, though a new ground, to be shared with Doncaster Rovers FC, was planned.

Jamie had hopes of going back. He still lived in the town, Louise was a Doncaster girl, and the fans had always been great with him.

People he knew, like Ray Green and David Prime, were still there. The fact that they were in the lower division was not an issue, despite his ambitions. Having dispensed with an agent, soon into 1996 he spoke himself to Dragons' chairman David Prime. "I told him that I didn't want a fortune and was prepared to accept a lot less than I had been on at the old club. I suggested a basic £250 a week, plus winning bonuses, and a half share of any future transfer fee if I moved on at the end of the first season. It was more than the other players were on, but could have been self-financing if it pulled in extra fans. He said that money was tight, but they wanted me to sign." There was no further contact for a while until coach Peter Regan got in touch after being pressed by some of the supporters. By then other clubs were showing interest. "I told him if a good offer came up I would have to accept it; I was a professional player." One duly did.

Doug Laughton at Leeds had said that he would keep in touch after the aborted 1994 transfer, and suggested that something might be available for Jamie in the future. However, in 1995 Laughton had parted with Leeds, and later returned to his native Widnes. So when he contacted Jamie in May 1996, it was with an offer to play for the newly renamed Widnes Vikings. "Some people didn't want him back in the game," wrote Laughton in his autobiography in 2003, "but he had paid for what he had done and that was it. I do believe that the laws of the land are laid down by the majority of the people."

Widnes were not in Super League. Despite being World Club Champions in 1989 and Wembley finalists as recently as 1993, they had hit financial difficulties of their own and had finished 14th of 16 in the old Stones Bitter Championship in 1994–95, two places and six league points ahead of Doncaster. That would have been enough to have avoided relegation under the previous system, but they were one of the aggrieved clubs left out to allow the inclusion of London Broncos and Paris St Germain in a reduced league of just 12 clubs. Instead they were in the First Division, where they finished seventh in the 1996 summer season. Jamie was more than happy to sign for them though. They may have fallen from grace, but were confident of a better future. A new, enthusiastic chairman, Tony Chambers, was at the helm, and a reported £300,000 sponsorship deal from ICI was in the bag.

"I was elated when Widnes came for me. One of the videos that Tony Lane had lent me back in South Africa featured Widnes, with

Martin Offiah, Jonathan Davies and the rest. Doug Laughton was a good coach; he had a presence, and I respected him from our negotiations at Leeds. Other clubs were talking about trials, or signing me for the reserves, but at Widnes I was wanted straight away. I needed to be playing – that was my job after all." Even though the club was hard up, they had no qualms about paying him the £250 a week he needed. Laughton moved upstairs to become football manager soon afterwards, leaving the coaching in the hands of Bernard Long, father of Sean, which made no difference to Jamie. Super League could wait, and maybe he could achieve it with the Vikings.

The ban still has six months to run, but Jamie agreed to start training at Naughton Park, which was being transformed by a multi-million pound redevelopment into the present stadium. The old stands had been flattened, with spectators on matchdays at the two ends. The deal was announced almost immediately. "Widnes have signed Jamie Bloem," reported *The Independent* on 29 May, "even though he is serving a 2-year suspension for drug abuse and will not be able to play until next season."

There was some quibbling from Doncaster. "Disgraced Bloem has let us down," hissed the headline in *Doncaster Star Sport* on 12 June. "Doncaster Dragons today accused disgraced former star Jamie Bloem of turning his back on the club as he prepares to hit the comeback trail," the article began, adding that the news of him joining Widnes had come as a big disappointment to Dragons fans who were hoping he would remain loyal to the club that had given him his break in British rugby league. Chief executive Bob Fox was quoted as saying. "Jamie Bloem promised he would telephone coach Peter Regan before he signed for any other club. He had definitely been approached by Peter but Bloem did not keep his word because the telephone call never came." That was not how it happened and he hit out at the allegations, his side of the story being printed on 18 June.

Regular trips over to Widnes allowed him to get back into gym work and other bits and pieces. He was still living in Doncaster, so the club put him up at the Hillcrest Hotel in Widnes at weekends, with Louise, so he could train on the Saturday and watch the games on the Sunday. "They did the same for us once I started playing," says Jamie. "It was a modern, premier hotel, and we thoroughly enjoyed it." The club started paying him, and treated him well. "They were outstanding. They looked after us really nicely." They also gave Louise a job in the office.

Jamie had been training at Thornesians rugby union club for three or four months before the ban was due to end in November. The rugby league season would be over by then, so he would not be able to get straight back into playing at Widnes. "Thorne was a little village in the middle of nowhere, but not far from Doncaster. One of the Dons fans lived there and got the coach to ring me." He began helping coach Howard Wilson, not coaching, but passing on tips to the kids. "Howard had been very impressed with how Wigan had played in recent cross-code challenges against Bath, and in the Middlesex Sevens, and like other coaches believed there was a lot to learn from league." The contract with Widnes was just for the league season, leaving him free to do what he liked for the rest of the year, so after November he took advantage of the new rules on professionalism to play three or four games with Thornesians to further help him get fit. "It was a nice field, and a good set-up with six or seven pitches. But they were a poor team in a lowish league. I played inside centre, and didn't get much ball."

Raring to go now, he was keen to make a start with Widnes, where the 1997 playing season kicked off on 26 January with a Challenge Cup third round encounter against Bradford amateur outfit Clayton. Some doubted he would be able to play well enough without the drugs, but that was never an issue for Jamie, whose form had been fine before he encountered them. Getting into the team was not automatic though. He still regarded himself as a full-back, and that position was already sewn up by the highly rated Gary Broadbent. So he was happy to be picked as a substitute for the Clayton match. The team was: Gary Broadbent, Phil Kendrick, Danny Myler, Boycie Nelson, Peter Smith, Phil Waring, Ben Lythe, Craig Makin, Jim Cassidy, Lee Hansen, John Harrison, Paul Myler, Gareth Cunningham. Substitutes: Jamie Bloem, Andy Collier, Paul Mills, Ian Connor.

Jamie took the field in the 32nd minute as a replacement for Gary Broadbent, and made an immediate impact with "a 50 metre break from the back with his first touch of the ball" according to the *League Express* match report. In selecting him as the 'Game Star', Chris Moore added that "his mere presence on the field was enough to raise the tempo." A try in the 79th minute was the icing on the cake as Widnes won 56–2. Doug Laughton was impressed. "I was very pleased with his performance," he told reporters after the game. "He looks as though he can do the business. He did as many drives as the forwards."

He remained on the bench for a while, despite continuing good displays. "Bloem is perhaps the most dangerous runner Widnes have," opined Andrew Kirchin in *Widnes World* on 12 March. The sale of Gary Broadbent to Salford for much-needed cash at the start of April gave him the chance to make the full-back spot his own. Coach Bernard Long was sure that Broadbent could be replaced. "Jamie Bloem has been outstanding in the past three or four games," he said, "so we shouldn't feel Broadbent's loss too much."

Jamie was also keen to atone for past misdemeanours and make an impression off the field. Widnes was a part-time outfit, training on Tuesday and Thursday evenings as Doncaster and Oldham had done, leaving time during the day. He and Ben Lythe spotted a local school team training and offered their assistance, watching them in matches and helping develop their skill levels. Later Jamie worked with Lunts Heath Lions under–16s, and was presented with their framed team photo as a thank you. If there were presentations to make, stores to open, or celebratory balloons to release, Jamie became the man. He got involved with the club's schools coaching programme around Widnes and Runcorn, running six-week courses in primary schools with the help of the club's apprentices. It was the sort of thing he had done in Doncaster. "I enjoy getting involved with the supporters," says Jamie. "Too many professionals don't like getting their hands dirty, but the supporters pay your wages."

There was even a Jamie Bloem Summer Coaching School. It was part of the club's initiative to spread the word about rugby league to Halton youngsters, and though it was named after Jamie, involved coach Graeme West and other first team players. The club wanted a name to put to it, and because he had won a few man-of-the-match awards and had a bit of a reputation as a crowd-pleaser – "I used to over-celebrate and jump into the crowd when I scored," – they chose his. "Places for this event were snapped up in record time!" said the advert in the club matchday programme for 30 July. "If you were lucky enough to get a place, don't forget to turn up on Monday 11 August at 10am. Please bring old clothes or training gear with your special Summer School T-shirt." Held in the park near the ground, it attracted

130 youngsters, aged between eight and 13, on that first day. "It's a rugby place is Widnes," explains Jamie.

There was a message to send out about drugs as well. The issue was not about to be instantly forgotten, journalists questioning him about it and rival supporters being quick to taunt him with it. Opposing players were fine. "At the end of the day it's a profession and the other players treat me as a fellow professional," he told *Super League Week*, "but their fans give me lots of stick." They still do – playing for Stainland amateurs in 2011 he was still hearing comments about "druggies". He quickly learned to laugh it off. "The more they jeer me, the better I play."

He had no intention of ever using drugs again though, and was keen that youngsters should not follow his previous bad example. Ray French reported Jamie's comments to youngsters at a Widnes training session in the *Rugby Leaguer*: "Stay away from drugs. You can get strong, if you want, on weights. There are other ways of having fun, other ways of becoming a better person than using drugs or steroids. That is not the way to go." On his visits to schools he found himself asked about it. "Although I don't go out of my way to bring the subject up, I'm happy to address any questions they might have," he said to Steve Fox in *Super League Week*. "I'm prepared to tell them straight out what happened and how wrong it is."

He was regularly tested. Whenever the testers appeared at games, two players would be randomly selected, but for Widnes the form always specified "Bloem and one other." This continued after he moved on, and always made him nervous, even though he knew he was clean.

Now established in the team at full-back, Jamie was appointed captain in mid-April. "It's a major honour for me," he told John Huxley in *League Express* at the time, and it goes to prove that you can be a useful player again after serving your punishment for breaking the rules." Widnes had asked him to think about being club captain when he first joined, but he felt it was too early for him. He had to concentrate on putting his game back together. "Doug Laughton asked me to take the job on when Phil Waring was dropped. Besides my responsibility on the field, I also sit in on selection."

It was not to be an auspicious debut as skipper, at Keighley in what was only his fourth start for the club. He limped off injured in the 24th minute of a 54–6 thrashing. Indeed the team were not playing well at all, the Keighley defeat being one of eight in succession. After beating Clayton in the Challenge Cup, they had bowed out the following week at Featherstone. But that defeat allowed entry to the Plate, a new competition for fourth round losers. The final was to be at Wembley as a curtain-raiser to the main event, a prospective great day out for players and fans, and a chance for the club to make some money. York and Bramley were beaten, with a home draw against Hunslet in the semi-final, only for another dreadful performance to bring the dreams crashing down in a 19–18 defeat. The Plate, which seemed to reward losers, was widely criticised, and it was not repeated.

Instead of appearing at it, Jamie arranged for the team to go away to North Wales together for a day over the Wembley weekend. "We need to start growing together as a team and a few days in each other's company must help," he told the press. The wives and girlfriends went along, a barbecue was organised, and there was a bit of training. "I don't remember exactly where we went," he says, "but it was on the coast, Holyhead way I think, because we had a run on the beach." It had little effect as the poor form continued, Widnes eventually finishing in 10th place out of 11, with only six wins from 20 league fixtures. Crowds were down – ground capacity had been reduced anyway because of the building work, and four matches had to be moved to Runcorn's ground at Canal Street; just 893 attended a midweek game against Rochdale there.

"Widnes had no money around that time," says Jamie. "It was a difficult time for them. We had a pretty poor team really. One of the overseas players, Brian Jellick, had a broken leg when he came and never played. Boycie Nelson, a centre from Wests Tigers reserves, played, but I thought he didn't like the big hits much, though he later won representative honours with New Zealand Maori. Ben Lythe, the other New Zealander, was a classy half-back though. Gareth Cunningham, Keiron's cousin, played, and Paul Myler. Sean Long, when he came, was a class above."

Long arrived from Wigan in April as part of the deal that took prop Lee Hansen in the opposite direction. In his autobiography *Longy*, he is not too complimentary about the club, which he left two months later to join St Helens for £100,000, but did seem impressed with Jamie. "A lad called Jamie Bloem came in and started playing pretty well," he wrote.

A try for Widnes against Barrow Border Raiders at Craven Park in the
Challenge Cup, February 1998. (Photo: Darrell Cooper).

Passing on skills – coaching local school students in a
Jamie Bloem Summer school at Widnes.

54

Jamie spent a time out of the team when he fractured a wrist at Featherstone. The club signed Steve Hampson to fill his spot, which meant playing at centre when he was fit again. There were lots of other new signings in an attempt to bring about a revival, including Australian Kyle White. "I've played against Kyle and have the bruises to prove it," he told the *Widnes Weekly News*. Unfortunately, existing players had to move out to make way, among them Ben Lythe.

At the end of May coach Bernard Long was replaced too, by former Wigan and New Zealand international star Graeme West, who had recently coached Wigan to a Grand Slam of all available trophies. Long took up a coaching role with the Academy side, while Dougie Laughton left the club. "I didn't have a good relationship with Graeme West. At his first training session, before he'd even introduced himself, he came into the changing rooms and said to me, 'You're not captain anymore!' Turning to Kyle White, he said, 'You're the new captain.' I'm a confrontational person. I'd rather people talk to me and tell me things. So I went to see him about it and we fell out. We never got on after that. He seemed to be finding fault with everything I did. It got so I hated playing for him, and I thought he hated me with a passion. It was a horrible relationship."

Both Laughton and Long had been pleased with his captaincy. Long had said in club programme notes that Jamie was relishing it and leading by example. "So long as he doesn't get too caught up in the emotion of it all, he should be a real asset to us in that role," he had written.

Results did not improve either, as the team slid towards relegation. A victory at Belle Vue against Wakefield Trinity with only two league games of the season left gave hope of avoiding the drop to Division 2. That win was not without its controversy; Wakefield players and particularly fans were convinced that the winning try, which was scored when Jamie's drop-goal attempt rebounded from a post into the arms of Kyle White, should have been disallowed for offside. At the time, the scoring team kicked off. After converting, Jamie was on his way back to the halfway line when referee Karl Kirkpatrick told him time was just about up and he would end the match after the kick-off, which was luckily towards the dressing room end. He asked if Jamie would see him safely off the field, with angry Trinity fans lying in wait. "Of course!" said Jamie, but when the whistle blew and Widnes had won, in the excitement he forgot the promise and joined his team-mates in racing to celebrate with the fans. Karl, meanwhile, was attacked near the changing rooms. "He had to spend the night in hospital," recalls Jamie. "It wasn't deliberate, I just forgot."

The last two matches were lost to bring relegation, but a few months later the gloom turned out to have been unnecessary when Widnes were reinstated in the First Division following a revamp of the lower leagues. The season ended with a strange Divisional Premiership in which clubs from Divisions 1 and 2 were divided into four pools of five, playing eight matches each. Widnes were in the Lancashire pool, but came next to bottom of that, so failed to qualify for the play-offs.

Despite such an unsuccessful season, Jamie had settled nicely. His own performances were sometimes spectacular. "Jamie Bloem produced a piece of magic to score a solo try near to the posts," wrote Chris Moore in *League Express* after a win against Swinton in August, while at Leigh later in the same month in the same publication, Mike Latham wrote that "Bloem burst over from 30 metres for a magnificent solo try," His exploits brought him the player-of-the-year award at the Supporters' Club annual presentations, a treasured moment. Plus he was chosen in the *Super League Week* Division One Team of 1997. "The South African has consistently been Widnes' most effective player, both in attack and defence," cited Steve Fox. He had scored 14 tries, and taken over the goal kicking when Sean Long left for St Helens – landing a total of 37 plus three drop-goals.

And he was happy off the field too: "Soon after arriving, Louise and I bought our first home in Widnes, a little detached two-up-two-down house, just round the corner from Stuart Spruce and Paul Howell, a Kiwi signed from Wellington Dukes. Both of them came round to ours a lot. Kyle White, a decent country and western singer, called a lot as well." It was a small community, much to their liking, where everyone knew each other. Another who visited was Bobby Campbell. "He was an Aussie country boy, who was the craziest person and a nice guy to have around. I used to keep snakes at the time. I had three, one of which was a boa constrictor. I was playing with it once when he called and he started teasing it. Well it launched itself at him and wrapped itself round him, getting tighter and tighter. Bobby turned white. We had to sit him down and calm him to get the snake to let go. The snake got so it could get itself out of the tank by vibrating against the cover.

Louise met it once on the stairs, and decreed that it had to be gone by 5pm. I managed it by about quarter to."

Louise became pregnant with Jordan during the summer, and there was no way she was having a child out of wedlock. She ruled that they had to be married by the end of the year. "I couldn't get December 31st," says Jamie with a cheeky grin, "so we opted for the 29th." A church wedding was out of the question because he had been married before, so they were married at the Everglades Park Hotel on the outskirts of Widnes. Missing out on a church ceremony became more of an issue later and they talked about having a marriage blessing. "I had a religious upbringing, as a Roman Catholic, like most British people in South Africa, though I was from a Dutch Reform (Afrikaans) area. I still am a bit religious, but don't enforce it on Louise and the kids." Their marriage blessing was achieved in December 2012 with a small ceremony for family and close friends at All Saints' Church in Halifax, where they had become worshippers.

Jamie arrived at the Everglades wedding at the last minute, after he and his best man, Royal Marine brother Drue, slept in after his stag night. For the evening do there were about 2,000 present, with rugby union and rugby league players galore. "Louise was not well and went to bed, so it turned into a bit of a bachelor party." The honeymoon was delayed until nine months later.

The rugby union representation at the wedding was because, by then, he was playing the game again. Off-season stints in the 15-man code were still all the rage, and Jamie's background made him an ideal candidate. There was interest from London Welsh, whose coach was Clive Griffiths; former Widnes star Andy Currier was already there. They were looking for a longer-term commitment though, and were based a long way away. "I'm a homely person and like to hang around where I live," he told *Widnes Weekly News*. So it was good news when a sponsor at Widnes rugby union club came to see him.

"He wanted me play for the club for three months, during the rugby league off-season, which I was more than happy to do. He then offered payment of £12,000! That was more than enough and I accepted straight away. Three cheques, for £4,000 each, were duly paid." The Wids were an ambitious club, keen for promotion from their league, North Division One, and had made several other signings. Jason Ashcroft, a back-row forward, came in from Leeds rugby union, stand-off Jason Gilbert from Waterloo, and the Hughes twins from Liverpool St Helens. Most of the players were paid far less than Jamie, but there was no animosity in the welcome they gave him.

He played on the wing, usually outside Hefin O'Hare, who he was to meet up with again later at Huddersfield rugby league. "Back in league we played the other way round, with me at centre," recalls Jamie. Widnes played a league style of game, quite successfully. "I enjoyed my stint there," he says. "There were a few league players, Gary Christie was one, and a couple of Kiwis, creating a strong rugby league-based side that used to hammer people."

One of the matches was a cross-code challenge against the Widnes league side to officially open their new stadium on the completion of phase 1 of the new development in November. "We played union in the first half, so built up a lead. The plan in the league half was for five drives, then set me up for a drop-goal. It worked three times.

"But I used to run with my mouth open, and paid for it when in a heavy tackle I bit through my tongue. I had it in my hand, hanging by a thread. The doctor put a few stitches in, and I went back on. Not for long. The stitches popped and it came out again. It was off to hospital for 47 stitches. I had to eat through a tube, and my mouth swelled up so I couldn't speak. I only missed two rugby union games though."

Jamie won himself selection for the Cheshire side in the County Championship, playing in a comfortable victory over Yorkshire at Wakefield RUFC. "I don't know why they played it there," says Jamie. "There were loads of better grounds in Yorkshire. It was always muddy, the changing rooms were old, smelly and damp, and the floodlights weren't brilliant either. It puts things into perspective a bit, playing on grounds like that." He was picked for the next game, but was called back to pre-season training at Naughton Park and had to withdraw, a disappointment for him in that Cheshire went on to win the championship, beating Cornwall in the final at Twickenham. The Wids were near the top of the league and he would have liked to stay on, playing for both them and the Vikings at the same time.

Yet despite everything not panning out exactly as he would have liked, for Jamie, and Louise as well, Widnes was still a fun place to be. "We hold it in our hearts," he says. "The people were great. We planned on staying at Widnes for several years."

But then Super League came calling.

8. Into Super League

The international part of Jamie's targets on returning to the game was achieved in November 1997 when he was chosen by the South African selectors for a short three-match tour of France. That was a golden moment. The other part, to get back into Super League, was soon to follow. The opportunity arose with Halifax – or Halifax Blue Sox as they were temporarily known.

In 2012, rugby league bosses, not to mention Super League clubs and their supporters, are quick to pontificate on how Championship clubs could not compete in the top division. Their fingers are no doubt pointed firmly at Halifax, deemed unworthy of a licence in 2011.

But Halifax were well able to cope, on the field at least, in the first seven years of Super League. They were founder members of it, even one of the very few stand-alone clubs in the original proposals for mergers. Third in the shortened 1995–96 transitional Centenary Championship, they had finished sixth in 1996 and seventh in 1997. Talk of franchises had added pressure, but the club's chief executive, Nigel Wood, was confident they would continue to make the grade. "We realise certain people within the game would like to see Super League reserved for big city metropolitan areas," he told *League Express* reporter Graham Clay in September 1997. "But we believe very strongly that if this game turns its back on strong, viable rugby league towns such as Halifax, then the competition will not be recognisable as rugby league."

Coach from March 1997 was John Pendlebury, who had succeeded Steve Simms. He had watched Jamie in action for Widnes and told him that he was interested. He promised to watch him again in the early part of 1998, saying that he needed a utility back, which was fantastic news for Jamie.

The season started with the Challenge Cup in February. The Super League season was not until April, so teams knocked out of the Cup were left with a break, but Widnes's First Division season kicked off on 8 February. It was an opportunity to impress Halifax, and his nine tries in 12 early-season appearances helped. Widnes were a slightly improved team following their reprieve from relegation, with attendances up in the partially complete stadium. Shane Wilson and Martin Moore, from South Sydney, were new oversees recruits, and a mini cup run saw victories over Oldham and Barrow before Super League side Salford Reds knocked them out in the fifth round.

John Pendlebury maintained his interest, Graeme West gave him permission to approach Jamie, and a meeting with Nigel Wood was arranged at Ainley Top at the end of March to sort out a contract. Terms were agreed, but then in Widnes's match at Leigh on 29 March he was injured. Leigh prop Tim Street dived to set up a quick play the ball and hit his head on Jamie's shin. "I thought I'd broken my leg, and was carried off," says Jamie. John Pendlebury rang asking him to wait until he regained fitness, which he was able to prove in further appearances for Widnes. He finally signed a two-year contract for Halifax on 5 May, providing him with financial stability for the first time since Doncaster. Fringe players Damien Munroe and Kevin O'Loughlin moved in the opposite direction as part of the deal.

"Halifax Blue Sox have confirmed the signing of utility back Jamie Bloem from First Division Widnes," reported the *Halifax Courier*. Football manager David Hobbs was relieved to get the matter resolved and was said to be looking forward to Jamie making a big impact at the club. "It's a step in the right direction as far as strengthening the squad is concerned," he said, "and we are delighted that everything is finally settled. Jamie has caught John Pendlebury's eye along the way and he told me to go out and get him. What we have is a complete player who will slot straight into a position where we have been a bit thin, while letting two players go who are still not the finished article."

Over at the renamed Halton Community Stadium, Widnes coach Graeme West was content too. Munro and O'Loughlin debuted against Rochdale Hornets, playing well. "I'm happy with the deal," said West.

Halifax had won four of their first five Super League games, with a strong team built around a powerful front row of Karl Harrison, Paul Rowley and Kelvin Skerrett, backed by Gary Mercer, Des Clark and Martin Moana. Gavin Clinch and Chris Chester were a fine, creative pair of half-backs, and outside them were Fereti Tuilangi, Daio Powell, Martin Pearson, Damian Gibson and David Bouveng. Others figured – Carl Gillespie, Richard Marshall and Simon Baldwin in particular – but it was a remarkably settled team that suffered few injury setbacks. Six players never missed a match – neither did Jamie once he had joined – and the others were rarely absent.

A rare disappointing moment in Halifax's successful 1998 Super League season. From the left: Jamie Bloem, Chris Chester, Karl Harrison, Daio Powell, Gary Mercer, water-carrier Andy Hobson, Paul Rowley, David Bouveng, Des Clark and Kelvin Skerrett.

Halifax team 1998. Jamie is second from the right, back row. (Courtesy *Halifax Courier*).

Gavin Clinch became a key figure, with the skills to turn a game. He gained a reputation for being able to steal the ball in a tackle, so much so that in some opposing teams, players were fined if he got the ball off them – but he still did.

The team were a close unit, with real camaraderie and a bond with each other. Jamie quickly became part of it, though provoked a few raised eyebrows at first. Des Clark tells of how at an early training session the players were heading off in the cars, Jamie still with his Widnes vehicle with his name on the side. "I thought I'd go with the new bloke. Gibbo and Clinchy were there. He was telling Gibbo, 'You're a defensive player and I'm an attacker; you do the defending and I'll score the tries.' As we got to know him more, we saw a lot of it was tongue in cheek, but he was always a confident bloke."

His debut was at Warrington. "We played in that horrible purple kit we had at the time," says Jamie. Shirt numbers were already allocated, but he was given a choice of those unused and opted for number 26. "I'd never had a squad number before, but I was 26 years old, and my birthday was 26 May," he explains. "I always tried to keep number 26 after that. I had a year at 12, and Gary Mercer insisted on number 2 one season, but otherwise I was 26."

The team at Warrington was: Damian Gibson, John Bentley, Fereti Tuilagi, David Bouveng, Daio Powell, Chris Chester, Gavin Clinch, Karl Harrison, Paul Rowley, Kelvin Skerrett, Gary Mercer, Carl Gillespie, Martin Moana. Subs: Martin Pearson, Jamie Bloem, Des Clark and Andy Hobson.

Coach at Warrington, who were second from the bottom of the league at the time, was Jamie's old boss Darryl van der Velde, so there was the opportunity to prove a point. The match was close-fought, boiling over on occasions. Jamie entered the fray just before half-time when John Bentley, himself just returned after completing a winter spell in rugby union on loan at Rotherham from Newcastle, left the field with a knee ligament strain. While the volatile nature of the match would have suited his style, he "had few running chances" according to Ian Rushworth's match report in the *Halifax Courier*. Warrington led 21–20 with 10 minutes to go, but the sending off of Karl Harrison for a "dangerous tackle" on Lee Briers turned the match decisively their way, even though they were down to 12 men themselves following the dismissal of Jonathan Roper. Halifax lost 31–20.

They were soon back to form, finishing an impressive third in the final Super League table behind Wigan and Leeds, seven points clear of fourth-placed St Helens. The final league game was a 42–0 thrashing of Leeds, still the only time Leeds have been nilled in Super League, but Halifax lost to them on their patch the following week in the first round of the inaugural play-offs, and crashed out at home in the second-chance match against St Helens 37–30 five days later.

It was a hugely disappointing end to the season. The 1998 Halifax team was to turn out to be the best Jamie ever played in, and should have won something.

In the utility role that John Pendlebury had wanted, he played full-back, wing and centre, scoring nine tries and five goals in 21 appearances. A highlight was a hat-trick from the wing versus Sheffield Eagles at The Shay on 6 September, which impressed his coach. "Jamie showed his sharpness which gets better with each game he plays for us," he said in the *Evening Courier*. "He is doing well at the moment and he seems to be growing in confidence from week to week."

Like at Widnes when he went there, parts of The Shay were also a building site. Halifax had moved there only weeks before, having left their previous ground at Thrum Hall, home for 112 years, in a quest for better facilities. The Shay, used by Halifax Town Football Club since 1921, was slowly being rebuilt. Very slowly – it was still unfinished when he retired. The old main stand remained in place while work continued on the construction of the South Stand. Training, now during the day since all the Halifax players were full-time on the back of the money from Sky Television, was up at the old ground at the top of Hanson Lane, still there pending its sale. It was to be some years before a deal was finally concluded to build an ASDA supermarket and bowling green on the site. Although that was bad news for the club in financial terms, it provided a useful base for the players. It continued to be used for second team matches, the kit was stored there, and it was from where the bus departed for away fixtures. The cricket field alongside could also be used for practice.

"Skerrett and Chester didn't train much," says Jamie. "It was their job to make lunch in the old kitchen in the pavilion; chicken pasta, carbonaras and so on. We ate it in the old board room, which still had that fabulous carpet with the club coat of arms. It was great there. Our cars got vandalised a bit though, and there always seemed to be something burning or smashed when we arrived." The ground was in a sorry state when it was eventually demolished. Leaving it was sold as a big thing to the players, the making of the club, but it was not to turn out quite like that.

Once Thrum Hall was gone, training became a perennial problem. A gym was built at The Shay, but the field was for the most part out of bounds. "We moved round a lot after Thrum Hall. Savile Park, Old Rishworthians for a while, Ovenden Park a bit, and the football pitch at Spring Hall before the new athletics track was laid. It was poorly organised in those days." There was also hill work at Shibden Park or further away at Oldham. "We'd all cram in to one or two cars, and have to roll out when we got there." The players all had to buy bikes, on which there would be three to four hour rides, Tuesday mornings during the season, and Saturdays before it. "Gary Mercer had the best bike – he always had to be the best; he fell off once trying to get past us and missed a game through it."

Jamie was still living in Widnes, travelling over with the Lancashire contingent – Simon Baldwin, Paul Rowley, Richard Marshall and Craig Dean. They took turns to drive, calling themselves "the Leigh bus", where the others all lived. "We used to meet up on the motorway at junction 19 near Birch. Once on the way home Craig Dean drove past where I was parked up, and made me walk back. So the next day when I was driving, and he was last out of the changing rooms at Thrum Hall, we left him behind. He got a lift with John Pendlebury I think, but he never trusted us after that and stopped coming with us."

The travelling was costing too much though, so he and Louise decided to sell their Widnes home in Blair Drive and move with young son Jordan to one of Stephen Pearson's houses at Chapel Lane, Salterhebble. In the same row were Gavin Clinch and his wife at the bottom, Damian Gibson and Des Clark higher up, and the Goldspinks next door. Afterwards, Paul Davidson moved in with Brett Goldspink. All a bit like *Coronation Street* or *Neighbours*, with friends side-by-side. "We'd go on the Playstation in one of the houses, winner stayed on, loser to do a forfeit like running down to the shop in boxers to buy ice creams. It was the same with cards. One time when I lost I had to get a tattoo of a devil on my shoulder. I told Louise it was because I had always wanted one."

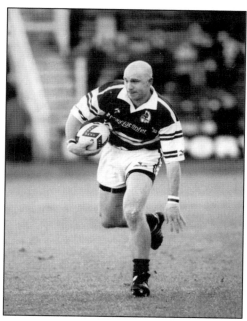
On the attack for Halifax at The Shay.

Martin Moana, like many of the others, was more of an outdoor type. "Bloemy and Gibbo were the Playstation freaks," he observes. "We were golfing one day, with a small wager of 50p a hole as we often did. Bloemy was having a shocking day. His phone went off and he pretended it was from Louise and he had to go. He still owes us that money."

Jamie, Louise and Jordan later moved on from Salterhebble, living in a cottage at Warley and, after coming back from a stint in France, another cottage at Hipperholme, until settling at Dudwell Lane, where daughter Isabelle came along in 2003.

Full-time coaching suited him. "I had a good rapport with John Pendlebury, and enjoyed working with him. He was up there on a par with Tony Smith as the best coach I played under. He was very much on the side of the players, tough but able to keep the harmony. There were no big motivational speeches, but you wanted to play for the guy. He'd been there, done that, the mark of a good coach. Those two that stood out for me were the ones that said least."

Training sessions would be very physical. "We trained hard, full-on bashing into each other, backs versus forwards. Some of us backs were big guys too, Freddie Tuilagi, Daio Powell and so on." One not so big was Damian Gibson; "I hid behind Freddie," is Gibbo's take on the activity. Pendlebury expected 100 per cent effort every session. "The discipline was there," comments Jamie. "We couldn't mess around so much on the coach back from away matches if we'd lost. Karl Harrison, as captain, played a big part. He sorted things out. When he left, and then John Pendlebury, that sort of discipline never came back."

Helping Pendlebury as conditioner was Steve Walsh, from Wigan. Steve was big on supplements. All the players were supplied with Tribustan, a legal steroid alternative. "They were big brown things in a big jar, like Smarties. We took eight or ten at a time, and had boxes of them to take home, so we might be having 50 a day. We also had Creatine, which was designed to supply energy to all cells in the body, but was primarily to gain muscle mass. There were protein shakes as well, Jaffa cakes, and Haribo sweets. "We had four packs of sweets on game day, including one just before the game and one at half-time, to give us a sugar high."

The Tribustan and Creatine bothered him a bit in view of his past. His regular drugs tests had ended, but still occurred occasionally. "I mentioned it to John, but everything had been checked out by the club." Although Tribustan has since been banned, it was quite legal then. The club soon found that a similar product, Tribulus, could be bought more cheaply from Bulgaria. But then came a shock when one of the players, Daio Powell, tested positive. "I panicked. I thought about contacting the Rugby Football League and explaining what it was and where it came from." But the club spoke with the RFL themselves, the stuff was checked, and the batch found to be contaminated. No action was taken against anyone, and they continued with the supplements.

It had been the same at Widnes, where someone associated with the club could always come up with any pills – all legal – that the players wanted.

Did they work? "Maybe, but not like the proper stuff did," says Jamie.

Little did he realise that problems of a different sort were just around the corner.

9. The Lee Briers episode

"Apart from Lee Briers' arm, what else do you like to eat?" It was a Mrs Merton-style fun question from team-mate Andrew Dunemann for his weekly column in the *Halifax Evening Courier* in August 2001. Dunemann had not been around at the time of the Warrington match in June 1999 – he arrived a few weeks later – but had picked up on the banter from the rest of the players. The incident where he was accused of biting Lee Briers in that game had become a big laugh for them, but it was anything but for Jamie at the time.

The season that for Jamie was to come crashing down at Warrington's Wilderspool had even begun ominously. One of the pre-season friendlies was at the McAlpine Stadium against Huddersfield on New Years' Day for the Infirmary Cup – and Jamie was sent off. He had been sin-binned in the 49th minute for arguing with referee Karl Kirkpatrick, was penalised two minutes after his return for allegedly punching, then within another minute sent off for his part in a supposed spear tackle on Huddersfield stand-off Craig Weston. Halifax were still in the game at the time, and fell away to lose 28–10, so it was irritating. "Danny Fearon made the tackle with me, and we both pulled out, so it wasn't a spear tackle." It was his second dismissal, following his indiscretion with Mike Kuiti while at Doncaster and was to be followed by another with South Africa in 2000, but despite his record he was later cleared of any offence at his hearing. However, if there were any thoughts of a better relationship with the disciplinary committee, they were to be proved premature not long afterwards.

Soon after the match the players jetted out to the La Santa, Lanzarote, for pre-season training. Jamie pulled his groin muscle, which turned out to be a hernia again, but recovered to become an ever-present in the first 15 matches. It was a less successful season for Halifax. Despite their performances in 1998, they had not actually won any trophies, and John Pendlebury was keen to make a few changes. Controversially he chose not to renew the contract of skipper Karl Harrison, and also replaced Daio Powell and Martin Pearson, while Fereti Tuilagi was lured away by St Helens. Paul Broadbent, Nick Pinkney, Graham Holroyd and Daryl Cardiss were among the replacements.

The season did not start well when Warrington narrowly won the first match at The Shay, and although Wigan were beaten 19–8, there were defeats at Gateshead and Sheffield among others, and a devastating 70–22 loss at Headingley against Leeds. Jamie, now alternating between centre and second row, had scored four tries, and kicked a few goals in the injury absence of Graham Holroyd, but it was a disappointing time.

Serious problems were developing behind the scenes; rumours of financial difficulties turned into reality when pay cheques began to bounce. Crowds had slipped below 5,000 with the poorer performances, and the wages of the leading players were high, fuelled by expectations raised in 1998. "Other clubs took it as read that the club was going out of business," David Hobbs told the press. Wigan Warriors homed in on key half-backs Gavin Clinch and Chris Chester and "several clubs have contacted members of the squad," said Hobbs.

In June Chris Caisley at Bradford Bulls brought up the idea of a merger again, which had been ditched amidst furious opposition from Halifax fans four years earlier. "I am not talking of a takeover," he said, "but the stark truth is that you cannot live in the past." There was also speculation of a merger with Huddersfield Giants, or even standing down from Super League to save money. Halifax company secretary Alan Lightowlers was quick to rule all this out. The sale of the old ground at Thrum Hall was proving troublesome, but it was hoped that could be resolved and part of the proceeds used to help sort out the difficulties. Some of that money, however, had been earmarked for building work at The Shay – club officials claim that everything they were supposed to pay in this respect was indeed paid. Substantial borrowings were made from Yorkshire Bank, which had security on Thrum Hall.

"We knew there were problems," says Jamie, " but John Pendlebury was a players' coach. He shielded us from stuff like that, and sorted out things with the directors himself."

On the field, the match against St Helens at The Shay on 30 May had brought four separate flare-ups and a summons for both teams by the RFL's board of directors to a hearing at Red Hall.

Against this background, the team travelled to Wilderspool to play Warrington on 4 June and an encounter for Jamie with Lee Briers.

He was tackled at one point by Briers, who a play or two later ran to the touch judge claiming to have been bitten. The match was being televised by Sky Sports, so there was more evidence that usual. Briers' arm could be seen over Jamie's mouth, but there was no proof of a bite... because there wasn't one. Jamie had been wearing a gum shield, so the bite marks that Briers showed to referee Steve Ganson were not his. The incident was placed on report and Jamie thought little of it.

His team-mates asked him about it at the end of the game, Jamie insisting on his innocence. They had seen the replays on the big screen, and again on television when they got inside, the camera angles making the incident seem incriminating. The national press saw the same pictures and pronounced him guilty, and the RFL ruled that there was a case to answer.

"I don't like Lee Briers as a person because of this incident," comments Jamie. "I was a guy with a chequered past trying to rebuild my career. I maintain that I didn't bite him. I like to think I didn't play dirty, although obviously I niggled a bit. I talked to them in tackles, pinched them a little, but I didn't bite people."

Yet the disciplinary committee managed to find him guilty. David Hobbs went with him to the hearing, at which they were not allowed witnesses. "Briers should have been at the hearing," Hobbs afterwards told the *Halifax Courier*. They were shown no clear evidence of bite marks. "It's like hanging somebody for murder without finding the body," he added. "It was 1 minute 20 seconds before Briers spoke to the referee. If it was a court of law it would have been thrown out through lack of evidence."

Though not present in person, Lee Briers had submitted a written statement, which was supported by a letter from the Warrington club doctor.

The committee then meted out a three month suspension, effectively the 17 matches that Halifax had left that season, plus a £250 fine. "I feel aggrieved about that," complains Jamie. "I was not guilty, and I was given a ban way in excess of what other players have received for that offence."

Press coverage before the hearing might partly explain how the disciplinary committee reached their verdict. It included quotes from a senior RFL official, who praised Briers for his actions in putting his complaint in writing. "I applaud that," the official said. "He has shown a responsible attitude."

While Briers was being praised, Jamie had his past record to contend with.

John Ledger in the *Yorkshire Post* of 9 June, the day after the hearing, reported that it was the third occasion on which he had been accused of biting in the last 16 months. "He allegedly bit Hunslet Hawks forward Rob Wilson while playing for Widnes Vikings last year, but though the RFL executive panel decided he had a case to answer, he was subsequently found not guilty. RFL officials also expressed their concerns to Halifax coach John Pendlebury following another allegation of biting by Bloem during a Super League match earlier this season after video evidence of the incident had proved inconclusive." Jamie, however, does not recall anything being said about any such incidents.

An appeal seemed the way to go. After the hearing, Briers submitted photographs of the bite marks. Halifax asked that they be examined closely, and depending on the outcome of that, would then decide whether to challenge the guilty verdict or the severity of the sentence. "It seems very strange they produce photos now," Hobbs told the *Courier*, "but they were not used in the original hearing when they should have been made available." He added that Briers had got his girlfriend to take pictures of his arm after the match, and was stung into submitting them when the Blue Sox claimed there was no hard evidence.

A day or two later a solicitor rang offering to fight the case for him, but by then events were moving on, and new doors opening, which made that no longer the route to take. He was contacted by Dave Ellis, a Castleford lad with a rugby league background, who was with the Racing Metro Rugby Union Club in France – in Paris. He was later to become France's defence coach, a role he still held at the 2011 World Cup. His suggestion was that Jamie switch back to rugby union and join them. He knew about the suspension, it was the reason he had called; he wanted a couple of robust rugby league players to boost his team. Jon Scales, who later had a spell at Halifax but then a former Bradford and Leeds player with a background in union, was going too, along with Stuart Power of Harlequins RUFC. The contract money would be way above what he was on at Halifax. It seemed too good to be true really.

70

As if to make up his mind, the Halifax club then sacked him. "That was a disappointing decision as well," he says. "They should have stood by me." But in the financial plight they were in, they no doubt felt they had to; it was nothing to do with any moral stance or belief that he was guilty.

The team missed him. He had been joint top, alongside Gavin Clinch, of the *Evening Courier's* "Star Man" player of the season table on seven points from two man-of-the-match performances and one third place. "The dejected centre's performances have been one of the few plus points of this season," wrote Matthew Finn. Then, after the team's defeat in the next match, "Bloem's absence was sorely felt in Wednesday's defeat to Wakefield at The Shay."

Gavin Clinch and Chris Chester were soon on their way to Wigan, followed later by David Hodgson, while coaches John Pendlebury and David Hobbs resigned.

But it was France for Jamie now. That was a better option than fighting the RFL, or Halifax, and by the following Friday he, Louise and Jordan were on a plane to Paris.

Jamie the golfer.

Looking for an opening, with Gary Mercer in support
(Photo: Keith Hamer)

10. France

The set-up at Racing Club was pretty good. "They flew us out there, wined us and dined us for a day, took us around the area, and showed us the ground, Charlety Stadium. We met Eric Blanc the president, found out that the stand-off was French Union star Franck Mesnel, that legend Serge Blanco was a director, and the coach was Jacques Feroux." It was ideal, even before it came to the contract.

Everything was written in French, but John Daniell, a New Zealand player at the club, could speak the language quite fluently and went through it with them. At the bottom were the terms, 50,000 francs a month net of tax (about £5,000), 8,500 francs a month for an apartment, and a car of their choice from sponsors Volvo. "We were told it was non-negotiable, either sign or it's gone, but we weren't going to turn that down. I did ask if they could throw in some return flights back home, and they agreed on six."

The club was well served by sponsors and backers. Another was sportswear clothing business Eden Park, which had been set up by five of Racing Club's players, including Eric Blanc.

Daniell later wrote a book on his experiences in France – *Confessions of a Rugby Mercenary* – and mentioned that Racing's organisation was borderline comic at that time. He noted that Jamie was paid more than him, an established player.

Racing Club had a long, proud history, having been established in 1882, but had just been promoted to the elite division after some years in the lower tier. They had become fully professional for the first time and did not have the personnel to play the flamboyant style that was common in France. There were a number of young French prospects, together with an overseas contingent that included three Romanian internationals, a couple of South Africans and Kiwi Daniell. Their idea was to import a few big aggressive lads from England to bash through the middle – Jon Scales fitted the bill even more than Jamie as an 18 stone winger – though that was never really going to work at this level.

Franck Mesnel, who was the brother-in-law of Eric Blanc, had won 56 caps for France between 1986 and 1997, but he was now 38 years old and struggling. Consequently Jamie, instead of playing in the centre, soon found himself at stand-off. A number of games were lost, the club sinking into the bottom three or four. "The play was incredibly tough. I needed to wear a scrum-cap, because they'd fly in with their heads. And I got bitten loads of times – quite ironic as I was only there because I had supposedly bitten someone."

Most of the away games were in the south of France, reached by air. They would fly out of Paris on the Friday evening, stay Saturday night to party after the match, then home on the Sunday morning.

For home matches at Charlety it seemed to Jamie that the rugby was secondary to the spectacle. "It was part of our downfall." The spectators were noisy, and there were lots of them. The area council subsidised it, so there was no need to charge for admission and the 25,000-seater stadium would be full.

"The set-up was out of this world," says Jamie. "The structures and training facilities were like at Wigan. The changing rooms were huge, with our own cubicles. And the catering afterwards; there was ham and cheese and there would be hundreds of bottles of wine, with beer on tap at the side. Jon Scales liked that. There would also be red wine at half-time – it gave you energy they said. It's what they do, I couldn't get into that part."

The club were not full-time, so training was only an hour or so on Tuesday and Thursday nights, somewhat unsophisticated and rudimentary. The rest of the time could be spent sight-seeing. The apartment – a kitchen, lounge/dining-room and bedroom – was right in the centre of Paris, 200 metres from the Arc de Triomph and four streets from the Champs Elysees. They encountered a bidet for the first time. "I'd never seen one before, but it was great for washing my boots, and for Jordan to sail his toy boats."

The other English players were in the same block and they met each day to eat together. "We took turns to cook, though more often than not it was Louise," says Jamie. "Once when Jonathan Scales took charge he came back with a nice looking piece of meat, but tough and chewy to eat. 'What is it?' we asked. 'Something called cheval,' he replied, not knowing that meant horse!"

They soon got rid of the Volvos, which proved inconvenient, replacing them with one small Clio for easier parking. "We left it in the street with the handbrake off, bumper to bumper. When people wanted to drive off they'd shunt the other cars forward or back to get out. The parking was expensive – it was cheaper to get a ticket, which usually we forgot to pay.

Arriving at the flat in Paris – Louise, Toni with Jordan,
Jon Scales and Stuart Power.

We travelled with one of the Romanians, a big, angry-looking fella called Roman Petrache, who didn't speak much English. One day when we went out he was sitting on the kerb giggling. 'Car gone,' he said. 'Truck take it. Funny.' To get it back we had to settle the parking tickets. The club paid, saying they'd take it out of our wages, though I don't think they actually did." They had other bumps and scrapes in the car, but it was a matter of swapping registration numbers and driving off. "Nobody ever does anything about it."

Jamie had a great time. "I loved it; it was a fantastic place to be." But Louise had quickly used up the six flights home and didn't settle. "Being so near the centre of Paris, it was still buzzing at 4 o'clock in the morning, and that summer was really hot." Louise found the language the biggest issue. "I didn't mind it when we moved from Doncaster to Widnes," says Louise. "I was excited going there, it was a new chapter for us, we were setting up a new home. But France was difficult. The language barrier was massive, so there were few friends. Jordan was 18 months old, but children weren't allowed on the grass in the park. Every month I'd fly back home to mum's with him for a week." The club agreed to release Jamie in December, and the family came home. It would be back to views of Wainhouse Tower instead of the Eiffel Tower.

"At the time I was negotiating a deal with another club, La Rochelle," says Jamie. "It would have set us up for life. France is the only part of my life where I have unfinished business. I would have loved to have stayed and finish it off. But sometimes family has to come first."

He reached his last game for Racing Club without having scored a try, but got two that day and kicked some goals to end on a high. The team itself slipped to the bottom later in the season and were relegated, but in 2001 merged with US Metro to become Racing Metro, playing at Colombes. More recent times have seen them become strong again, with appearances in the Heineken Cup.

For Jamie, having been paid two months wages in advance, there was £10,000 to survive on for a while. However, before they had even left France, Gary Mercer, now player-coach at Halifax, had contacted him to return to The Shay. There was interest from Salford as well, but despite the nature of his exit from the club the previous June, a return to Halifax was the perfect option.

11. Back to The Shay

Halifax appeared to have overcome their financial difficulties by selling a few of the leading players and entering administration. They were operating under a Company Voluntary Arrangement (CVA), making monthly payments towards clearing the debts, which allowed them to function much as before, and trying to rebuild. Andrew Dunemann had joined, and with the likes of Greg Florimo, Brett Goldspink and Gael Tallec arriving around the same time as Jamie, the team was looking competitive once more. They had finished the 1999 season in ninth spot of 14 clubs and hoped to progress. By 2002 the money troubles were to be back with a vengeance, but until then they remained a useful Super League outfit.

For Jamie, any remaining ill-feeling on his return was soothed by being in a position to negotiate a new contract. "I was still aggrieved that Halifax had not stood by me, and I still felt they owed me money from June. My payments had stopped immediately the contract was cancelled, so I'd not received what I was due for the first part of that last month. So I held out for a three-year deal, worth £38,000 a year plus match payments. There'd be an extra £350 for an appearance, and a further £250 if we won."

Pre-season training was well under way by the time he arrived, but Jamie was fully match fit and he had timed it perfectly. "I got back just in time for the trip to Jacksonville in Florida, U.S.A."

Warm-weather training abroad had become the norm for Super League clubs, and still is for the more affluent ones. It provided an opportunity to get through work which could be impossible in the snow and ice of mid-winter England. Under John Pendlebury, Halifax had used Lanzarote's Club La Santa, claimed to be the world's number one sports and active holiday resort. With its fields, running track and other facilities, it was a popular venue for many professional sports' teams. "Conditioner Steve Walsh flew over early to sort everything out. It was all planned, even the meals. But he had a good tan by the time we got there." For Jamie, La Santa proved to be the most beneficial of all the pre-season camps. "It was hard work there. We had to do 40 lengths of the Olympic-sized pool every morning, there were video sessions afterwards, then morning and afternoon training outside."

But the club then used Jacksonville. There were plans at the time to spread the game to the United States, promoters over there offering financial support for teams to visit. The following year, 2001, Leeds and Huddersfield also went, to join Halifax in a tournament along with a U.S.A. selection, the Florida Sunshine State Challenge. "Leeds were booked into the same hotel, which they were not pleased about, and said we should move out because they had booked first. We weren't going to budge, so they ended up moving instead." In the 25-minute match on Saturday 3 February, Halifax lost 18–10 to Leeds, who went on to beat Huddersfield in the final. Jamie, and a few other front-line squad members, did not play.

"Jacksonville was more enjoyable because of where it was and what it was. One day on the 2000 trip they got us tickets for an American Football game, at the huge Alltel Stadium. Seven or eight of us went, paying $30 each towards it. The Jacksonville Jaguars were playing Miami Dolphins, who had superstar Dan Marino making his last appearance." Jacksonville won 62–7. "There was loads going on at the stadium, and afterwards nobody leaves. There were groups playing touch football outside; we joined in, quickly caught on to the rules, and won a few games. When they found out who we were, it attracted a bit of interest."

Like La Santa, Jacksonville had superb training facilities. "The gym work at Jacksonville University was good; they had weight rooms, and massive changing rooms with cubicles. We were also able to do a lot of work on moves there. But I think it worked best as a bonding tool rather than an opportunity for hard training."

Such a bonding trip was to a line-dancing night club, the Rusty Spur. "Jacksonville is a high-rise city on one side of the river, but on the other it's like the Deep South with pre-fabs and dusty roads. The Rusty Spur was on this other side. There was an all-you-can-eat buffet next door, where we went first, then to the club. We didn't fancy line dancing, so we started playing drinking games. When you were eliminated, you had to join in the line dancing. Brett Goldspink managed to knock an old couple over, but Marvin Golden took to it and was quite good."

Halifax had their share of players who liked to have a good time, which included plenty of drink. "The bath in the room shared by Luke Savelio and Marty Moana was full of ice and cans. Theirs was the card room for after training. Wherever I went in rugby league, there was always a card culture, usually led by the overseas boys. Like on the bus for away matches. In Jacksonville the games went on late into the night, with lots of money involved. I watched one of our forwards lose a four figure sum in one game – he wrote out a cheque to pay his debt." When money is involved, there can be flare-ups, and there were usually a few along the way. "I remember two players coming to blows when they'd had too much. The rest of us found it hilarious to watch because they were missing with their punches and kicks. In the end they both fell over – and fell asleep."

Jamie joined in with the cards, but was never a big drinker. "I'd have a few, but then go back to my room to watch films. Some of the others would be drinking until the early hours, causing problems the next day. "We had swimming sessions fixed for 6am each morning, and most of us were there on time, ready to get into it. There was a £100 fine for any who were late, but what was £100 with the contracts some were on? When someone went to get one particular player who was missing, his hand emerged from the bedcovers proffering his £100 instead."

Generally the trips had a beneficial effect. "It was good to be there," says Jamie, "but for the club it was a bit of a waste of money." When that money dried up, there was no pre-season trip at all one year, then the next it was in England, a few days based near Newcastle. "It was a bit farcical really, with nothing properly organised. We trained in a big park, near Newcastle United's ground."

After Jacksonville 2000, the first three league games were won, against Hull, Wakefield and Leeds, and though there were defeats along the way, Halifax were competitive. "There is never a problem with the spirit, and we work hard enough for each other at this club," Jamie told *League Express* after a home 28–24 defeat by St Helens in which he was named man-of-the-match. "But we are missing the technique of experienced players in vital positions, and we cough up too much ball. But we have deserved more from our last few games." The Blue Sox finished eighth, with 11 victories and a draw from the 28 fixtures, which would have been enough to reach the play-offs under the present system, though not in 2000. Jon Scales, his mate from France, turned out in one game in July, but Jamie himself was an ever-present until the last month when he dislocated his pelvis. He had scored six tries and 27 goals in 29 appearances.

He had also made the transition into the pack. He had been used as a second-rower by John Pendlebury a few times in 1999, but it became regular in 2000. "The 28-year-old has been a revelation since switching to the pack this season, wrote James Roberts in the *Halifax Evening Courier* in July. He fitted well into the aggressive style that Gary Mercer favoured in his early time as a coach. "Jamie is out and out class," enthused Mercer. "I knew right from the start that he was a back-rower and not a centre, full-back or winger. In the middle of the park he can channel that natural aggression he has for the good of the team."

The 2001 season was more of a struggle, but Halifax, still the Blue Sox, finished ninth above Salford, Wakefield and Huddersfield. Jamie played 23 times, scoring six tries and 44 goals. Having been a success in the second row, it was a surprise when coach Gary Mercer decided that he was to be a winger, allocating him the number 2 shirt rather than the number 26 he asked for. "It could be a long-term move for Jamie," Mercer told the *Courier* in January. "We have a lot of competition for places in the back-row this year with myself, Shayne McMenemy, Danny Tickle and Paul Davidson. But we are not overstaffed in the backs and I think that Jamie can be an asset for us out there. He is very good under the high ball and will add some aggression to our backline which perhaps we didn't have last year."

He made a good fist of it. "Bloem looks a reluctant winger at times," observed James Roberts in his summary of a Challenge Cup victory at Barrow in the first match, "but on a day when effort was more important than inspiration he excelled." He was "always on hand to take a forward drive and more often than not beat, or at least flattened, the first tackler." But his stay on the wing was to be short.

Following an early-season loss at Wakefield, Mercer resigned as coach, and soon also left as a player. "Gary had been shoved in at the deep end," says Jamie. "He was too passionate to be a head coach. He couldn't step back from being a player to running the team. He later became a defence coach at Glasgow Warriors rugby union, which was better for him." Mercer, keen on statistics, wanted the team to concede less penalties – the Blue Sox had been the most penalised side in Super League in 2000. "But some players went into their shells, afraid to make tackles in case they gave penalties away."

Halifax team in 2000. Jamie is second left, middle row.

On the way through for Halifax.

He was replaced by his assistant, Steve Linnane, who moved Jamie to centre for two matches before mainly using him from the bench. Jamie believes it would have been better for Steve to remain as assistant. "He'd been a good player himself in Australia, but I thought he struggled a bit with man-management. He took things too personally and got too emotional, and maybe in the end that lost him the respect of the players." The team's relative lack of success certainly rattled Linnane, who would go and sit on the coach after the match to brood about it. He was very upset at half-time in one match, complaining that the players' performances would cost him his job. Jamie, as skipper, encouraged him to get a grip.

For his troubles, he found himself dropped, and playing for the second team at Salford on 2 May. Also there was Jamie Thackray, a regular in the second team much to his annoyance. Thackray had blown up at a training session, claiming to be the best prop in Great Britain and that the coach should use him. Linnane consequently didn't.

The match at Salford almost got him into trouble again – again as an innocent party. Playing on the wing for Salford 'A' was Julian Penny, who happened to be black. During the game Jamie ran into him near the dug-outs, and as he went to play the ball, Julian accidentally stood on his hand. "It re-broke a previously broken finger, and I called him a stupid so-and-so. He told the referee that I'd called him a black so-and-so, and the incident was put on report. Julian's a nice kid, we shook hands when the match ended, and he might have misheard." However, the story that he was being investigated for racism made the press. "Me coming from South Africa made it worse, with their history of apartheid, but I'm not a racist. I've many black friends and friends from all other ethnic minorities."

Nothing more was heard about it until he was summoned to Red Hall, with the press again milling outside. But this time there was no case to answer. The touch judge, who had been a metre away from the tackle, said in his report that there had been no racist comment, and that he did not mistake what he had heard. The case was thrown out. "It was just ridiculous. There should never have been a hearing. You can still read about the accusation when you type my name into Google, and it's annoying."

In his anger he considered again whether he should pack the game in, but after time to think about it realised that was not the way to go.

"Its other people that make you controversial," he says. "It's not me. Coming back each time makes you strong, not controversial."

Jamie had become less of a front-line player since Gary Mercer's departure, a situation noted by his old club Doncaster. He knew little about it, but in November the Dragons approached Halifax to take him on a three-month loan – their Northern Ford Premiership season began on 2 December, three months ahead of Super League, and their team already included the former Halifax pair Martin Moana and Marvin Golden. Steve Linnane knocked back the bid, saying "Jamie is a contracted Halifax player and a member of the first team squad. Everyone is starting the new season on the same level." Doncaster's Elland-based chairman John Wright pulled out. "We were only interested in a loan," he commented. "Jamie is on a substantial contract with Halifax and we cannot afford those kind of wages.

The 2002 season indeed saw him restored to the starting line-up, and he came back strongly. "If his pre-season form is anything to go by, things could be looking up for Jamie Bloem," wrote James Roberts in the *Courier* on 2 March. "It is to his credit that he has stuck to his guns during the winter, and has, apparently, warmed to the challenge facing him."

Ahead of the Super League campaign Halifax were drawn away to St Gaudens in the Challenge Cup. For such trips, as with London Broncos and later Whitehaven and other ventures into France, there would be an overnight stop. Jamie generally roomed with Chris Birchall, a good friend, whose pre-match rituals used up the en-suite. Their room in St Gaudens overlooked woodland and Jamie, needing to relieve himself, used the balcony. Little did he realise that club officials Chris Murgatroyd and Sarah Morgan, with physiotherapist Helen Smith, were passing beneath; their consequent photographs embarrassingly found their way on to the office computers.

The match itself brought a good performance and a comfortable victory. Halifax then almost won at Warrington in the opening Super League fixture. With the scoreboard at 24–22 against and time running out, Jamie's confidence led to a bold decision to take a quick tap rather than kick for goal, only for the Wire defence to hold out and score again themselves to win the game.

Jamie's form held up. "Steve and I had our differences last year," he admitted in the *Courier* in April. "But I have been working hard, he has given me a chance and I am going to grab it with two hands. I had a problem with my pelvis last year as well and I couldn't walk the day after I played. But I had an operation in the off-season and that seems to have sorted it out."

For someone who plays like Jamie, injuries will almost inevitably be a problem. The pelvis injury had originated in Jacksonville in early 2000, running on the beach. "It was treated as a hernia and I kept playing, but I got whacked in a match against Hull and it turned out to be a dislocated pelvis. My pelvis was two centimetres out on the right, making one leg shorter than the other. I went for an operation at the end of the season, when BUPA fitted a fibreglass plate across the pelvis. I was laid up for three or four months during the off-season. It was very painful; I couldn't use my stomach muscles, couldn't walk, and Jordan was trying to jump on me when he came home from nursery. I had a bed in the lounge, Louise had to bathe me, and I got through a lot of on-line betting."

There had been the neck injury at Oldham – "I still get neck pain when it's cold" – the tongue cut at Widnes and there was to be a broken left leg at Huddersfield. "I've had broken fingers, collar bone, both hands, wrist, I've fractured my metatarsal a few times, had L4 and L5 fractures in my back without realising, which healed themselves, and had my medial ligaments done. But players today seem to be getting even more injuries. The supplements they're on, and weight programmes, are building muscle, but this is putting strain on tendons, joints and ligaments."

Unfortunately for Jamie and Halifax, results were no better in 2002 than they had been in 2001. "Training had become less demanding and physical," notes Jamie. "People got complacent," Not that his own form slipped too much. "Jamie blooms amid the chaos" was the *Courier*'s Star Man headline after a defeat at Leeds, and although Wakefield (twice), Widnes, Castleford, Warrington and Salford were beaten, it left a worrying battle against relegation towards the end. Fixtures against bottom two Salford and Wakefield Trinity among the last three matches always gave hope, but six consecutive defeats, culminating in a 64–0 stuffing at St Helens, was alarming. The Friday night loss at St Helens heralded a dramatic weekend in which an "advisory group" of local businessmen led by former Halifax Mayor Stephen Pearson moved in to help the board.

Jamie and Louise.

Left: Happy times with Dad in Australia.

Middle: Jamie the young athlete – leading a race in South Africa.

Bottom: In a team group in Craven Week, the South African rugby union annual youth festival.

On the attack for Doncaster against St Helens at Knowsley Road in the sixth round of the Challenge Cup in February 1994. Andy Gascoigne is the Doncaster player in support; the tackler is Tea Ropati.

Looking for an opening for Widnes against Swinton, in a home match played at Runcorn in 1997.

Left: In the traditional blue and white hoops of Halifax, 1998.

Below: Playing for Huddersfield. (rlphotos.com)

In action for South Africa.

Scotland team in 2004 with coach Steve McCormack.

Charging forward for Halifax against the Bradford Bulls.

Jordan (right) mascot at The Shay with friend Sam.

Top: Jamie with his mum.

Left: Jordan and Isabelle.

Below: Starting out in rugby union in South Africa.

Old Rishworthians: Winning promotion for the first time
Top: Celebration – Jamie cracks open the Champagne as promotion is won.
Middle: Acknowledging the applause. Bottom: Another goalkick from Jamie hits
the mark at the picturesque Copley Ground. (All photos: Mike Riley)

A massive shake-up, which included the ditching of the Blue Sox nickname, brought the dismissal of Steve Linnane as coach, only weeks after he had signed a new 12-month contract.

He was replaced immediately by Australian Tony Anderson, a hero locally from his time as a player in the great side of the 1980s and on the coaching staff under John Pendlebury. It seemed a good move, motivating players and fans alike with fresh enthusiasm. "He was the right man for the job," says Jamie. "We'd known that Stephen Pearson was trying to do something. The board of directors wanted the senior players onside, so I had been told that Tony would be coming." The next match at The Shay saw Warrington outscored three tries to two, and although Halifax were beaten 19–16, the signs of a turnaround were much in evidence.

That brought the crucial match at The Willows against Salford Reds, coached by Karl Harrison and featuring Damian Gibson and Graham Holroyd in their line-up. A press advertising campaign exhorted supporters to get behind the team, which, inspired by Gavin Clinch, roared into a commanding lead, suffered a jitter or two, but triumphed in the end 34–26.

With safety secured, Wakefield were beaten too, and the corner seemed turned. The players talked of sticking together, Australian centre Dave Woods of extending his stay, and Tony Anderson of building a team for the future based on talented young English players.

But the coach's ideas were stimulated by the club's need to save money. The proceeds from the sale of Thrum Hall had finally come through, but were only around £1.6 million, and went mostly to the Yorkshire Bank to discharge recent borrowings. Still in a CVA following the earlier financial crisis of 1999, the club was struggling to meet its repayment requirements and was building up new debts as well. It hoped to enter a second administration, to extinguish both problems. To do that, money owing to HMRC needed to be reduced to a point where the Inland Revenue could not block the second administration. "Stephen Pearson did the deal with Inland Revenue officers," explains Michael Steele, another advisory group member, "to leave us alone while we overpaid to reduce the debt to that figure."

The payments could be made by using much of the money received from Super League through the Sky contract. The office and community side of the club was slashed, but the playing budget had to take most of the hit, with the wage bill reduced to just 25 per cent of the money from Sky. Like at all Super League clubs, many players were highly paid. "I was on £38,000 a year, but five were on far more," says Jamie. "One was on £80,000, one £70,000, and the others up in that region. The rest earned £30,000 or below." The club had stretched themselves too far – and were in breach of salary cap regulations.

The total wage bill was below the salary cap maximum, but the rule that prevented payments to players in excess of 50 per cent of relevant income had been met by some of the funds from the Thrum Hall sale being included. This was later deemed by the RFL to be unacceptable and two league points were docked from the next season's record.

The points deduction was to be of little significance, but the consequences of the overspending, and the efforts of the new advisory group to get the club back on track, had a disastrous impact on the players and the club's Super League standing.

Called to a meeting, the six top earners were told they would have to take a 60 per cent cut. "I understood why they were doing it," says Jamie, "but you can't take a cut like that. As full-time players, we didn't have any other income. After tax I was getting £2,300 a month – the new deal would not have been enough to even cover my mortgage, never mind all other commitments and living expenses. I was up for getting Halifax out of the slump, and offered to accept a 25 per cent drop, which itself would have been hard. But the advisory group wouldn't budge on the 60 per cent.

"It was one of the saddest times of my career. I felt I was being shunted out. We were accused of being greedy for not accepting the cuts; the players on lesser money were told that it was us who were stopping the club surviving. 'These six players won't take pay cuts to help you guys have a club,' they said. Louise was having miscarriages around this time – she had five between Jordan and Isabelle. There was one going on at the same time as the meeting and I just thought, 'I haven't got time for this.' Even that was used against me, with a claim that I was using our misfortune to get money out of the club. Three Australian players went home, leaving their agent to sort out their dispute. I couldn't do that, so I decided to find another club."

12. Huddersfield

Still having no wish to work with an agent, finding a new club was down to Jamie himself. But any financial worries in the meantime were eased with an approach from Halifax rugby union club.

Their president, David Brook, a former boss at Halifax RLFC during the 1980's glory days, and coach Kevin McCallion, offered an opportunity to join them for the winter of 2002–03. Under Brook's sponsorship, they had started to pay some of their players and had surged through the regional leagues to reach National League status. Graham Holroyd was there, and going quite well as their top points scorer, as was Ben Anderson, son of Australian rugby league legend Chris. It was ideal for Jamie. "I was happy to keep playing. I enjoy going from one sport to the other; I like to keep going."

Jamie played 10 matches for the Ovenden Park club, scoring a try, five conversions, three penalty goals and a drop-goal. "I mellowed out in the rugby union a bit. I got about £300 a game; not a fantastic amount, but good enough for the off-season." The money came from a sponsor, Peter Smith at Feather Diesel, based at Lowfields Business Park at Elland. For a time, yet another promotion seemed possible, but after three narrow defeats in February the team slipped to a final position of fourth in National Three North – still their highest ever ranking.

Kevin McCallion was pleased with his displays. "It took him three or four games to settle in," he said in the *Courier* later, "but I was probably playing him out of position at full-back. By the time he left us he was causing plenty of damage. He also had a tremendous attitude in training, is a good influence on everyone else and is a good laugh."

Jamie almost ended up in the Scotland rugby union international side. Coach Ian McGeechan had often favoured players with a League background, notably Halifax's John Bentley when he had charge of the Lions tour of 1997. "Kevin McCallion had probably told him about my Scottish eligibility, and I was called into the 40-man squad as a crash-ball man at inside centre." Andy Craig, another former Halifax player, was also there.

"The selection left me with a decision to make. By that time my rugby league future had been sorted out, and I was required there. I picked rugby league, and withdrew from the Scotland squad. I might not have got near the team. Andy Craig took the centre spot and went on to do well."

His new rugby league deal was at Huddersfield. The Giants had endured a torrid time in Super League, four times between 1998 and 2001 finishing bottom, latterly under the coaching of Tony Smith. They had been relegated on that fourth occasion, allowing them to regroup in the 2002 Northern Ford Premiership. They had won it at a canter, allowing them to rejoin Super League in 2003 with fresh impetus.

Jamie's mate Jim Gannon had decided several months earlier to leave The Shay to become one of Huddersfield's first new recruits, and it was he who tipped off Tony Smith to speak to Jamie. "Tony asked me what the situation was and I told him it had all broken down with the board at Halifax. They were quick to release me when I asked, and I was off to Huddersfield." A year's contract worth £40,000 was more than he had been on at Halifax, even before the cuts.

"Jim and I bought an old Ford Fiesta together when we were at Huddersfield... we got on really well. From Ainley Top we used to drive down the old road which went through Fartown. Whoever was driving would try to freewheel from the top and see how far they could get in neutral. There were some tight bends and we'd be crawling along at three or four miles per hour, and traffic lights to negotiate, but I got all the way to the gym on Leeds Road once. Another time the front left wheel fell off and Jim had to drive the rest of the way on three wheels.

By the traffic lights in Fartown there was a house with two huge gold lions adorning the gate. Before one match I jumped out and touched each of the lions for luck. We won the game, so thereafter on game day we used to stop and both rub the lions' heads. The owners of the house noticed after a while and came out to wish us luck themselves.

The car served its purpose, but before the season was out had been stolen from a Halifax town centre car park and written off. Now that we're not playing together, Jim and I get on like a house on fire and our wives are good friends too. He's one of the nicest guys around." From up in the stands, the two looked similar. "People used to mix us up. I don't know why, I was a lot faster than him."

Squad numbers were allocated on the pre-season training stay at Ampleforth College. Most players had a preference, but second-rowers usually wanted 11 or 12 just as full-backs wanted number 1. Tony

Smith decided to draw lots where there was conflict, but had no problems when it came to Jamie's turn and he asked for his usual 26. "You've got it!" he said.

Tony was different from other coaches he had worked under, but soon won his admiration. The sessions were less about physical contact and battering into each other, but more on structures, where to stand, and agility work. "At Ampleforth there were war games, laser-quest type stuff in the woods, and orienteering, the first team back being excused from some task the next day."

A broken ankle sustained in a pre-season friendly caused him to miss the first few matches, including a shock defeat at Hunslet in the Challenge Cup. He was fit by the end of March, however, and finally able to make his Huddersfield debut from the substitute's bench at Belle Vue, Wakefield, on 6 April. The team that day was Marcus St Hilaire, Hefin O'Hare, Julian Bailey, Stanley Gene, Alex Wilkinson, Paul March, Brandon Costin, Darren Fleary, Darren Turner, Mick Slicker, John Grayshon, Steve McNamara, Jarrod O'Doherty. Subs: Jamie Bloem, Eorl Crabtree, Jim Gannon, Matthew Whitaker. Huddersfield won 14–10.

Other players around included Matt Calland, Graham Holroyd, Paul Reilly and Ben Roarty, plus youngsters Paul White and Iain Morrison. It was a decent if unspectacular side, which won 11 and drew one of its 28 fixtures, to finish tenth of 12 teams, acquiring the notable scalps of high-flying Wigan at McAlpine Stadium, and beating Leeds for the first time in 38 years along the way.

One of those below the Giants were Halifax, who had started well enough with a win in London, but then lost the next 27. Their self-imposed reduced salary cap had left them with too many inexperienced youngsters, and others who were not good enough, increasingly unable to compete.

"It was hard having to turn out against Halifax. I had mates playing for them, like Johnny Lawless. It was hard seeing them going through such strife." Halifax were one of the teams they met three times to make the fixtures up to 28. The first two were close, only a late Brandon Costin field goal ensuring a 21–20 success at The Shay and it was just as tense, 28–26, at McAlpine Stadium, but the third at The Shay in August finished 54–12.

Jamie played 22 Super League games for the Giants in 2003, scoring three tries and 11 goals, and coming top of the Opta stats for most marker tackles. "Bloem has been one of the most solid and consistent performers for the Giants this season," complimented Chris Roberts of *the Huddersfield Daily Examiner*.

He built up a good rapport with coach Tony Smith and his assistant Steve Deakin. Not long after he had arrived there, Louise suffered another miscarriage. "I hadn't said anything, but they could tell I was angry in training, and found out from Jim Gannon." They offered their support, with Deakin, a religious man, encouraging him to do something nice on his day off. "We took his advice and went up to Shibden Park with Jordan to feed the ducks. The next day, Deaks said he had been to Liverpool, seen the Bishop, and they'd said a prayer. He gave me a pendant and card that had been blessed with holy water, which stayed up on the mirror at home for years. I got emotional about it, that someone had taken the trouble to do that for me. In a game of tough men, he's a nice fella." The next pregnancy was daughter Isabelle.

He has similar views on Tony Smith. "He's not much older than me, but you wanted to give everything for him. Like John Pendlebury, he could just say the right thing. I remember the game against Wigan when we were losing at half-time. He got his chair, turned it round like always, and sat facing us leaning on its back. 'That's not as we've been training, is it. We know how to fix it don't we.' It was just enough. A buzz went round. We ended up winning 32–24."

Towards the end of the season Smith called him in to offer a new contract. He explained that he himself was leaving, but that everything could be sorted before he went. "I said I wasn't happy with that, that I would rather wait for the new coach and make sure I was wanted before I signed." When Jon Sharp took over, he phoned to introduce himself, and Jamie said he would be glad to play for him. "He told me that would not be happening, that he wanted a younger team." Sometime later the club's chief executive, his old mate Ralph Rimmer, contacted him to say a place had become available, as some had rejected their offers. "I asked if the money was the same, and he said it would be less, which made me feel they didn't really want me, so I turned it down. I'd just started my own business, so the idea was to concentrate on that, pack in rugby league, and maybe play a bit of union."

The business idea was quite a sudden thing. "I'd always been the handy sort, particularly outdoors, and creative. I'd just renovated my own garden, done a patio with a mate, and suddenly I knew what I wanted to do, become a landscape gardener. The physical side, digging out or carrying heavy materials, suited him well. "I bought a red 'Postman Pat' van, a few tools, and I was off. I've been busy ever since. I'll never be a millionaire on it, but it's okay."

It was touching for him to read a clutch of uplifting letters printed in the *Huddersfield Examiner* on 10 September, from supporters sorry to see him leave. "What a game Jamie Bloem had against Widnes," wrote DB. "He put in a sterling performance, one in my opinion worthy of another contract with the Giants. I find it hard to believe they are letting him go." John of Huddersfield said, "Come on Mr Rimmer, wake up and see what we are seeing, player of the season for me." CJ & CA thought "He has been a model professional this year and deserves another year at least," while Gerald Smith from Newsome believed "his attitude since he was told he was no longer required for next season has been 100 per cent."

The anticipated offer to go back to Halifax rugby union club, now more ambitious than ever, was forthcoming for the 2003–04 season. A couple of Samoans had been recruited, fly-half Dougie Sanft and Number 8 Rob Afoa-Peterson, plus an Australian wing forward David Jessiman. Half the squad was still from Calderdale though, and most of the others from within a 30-mile radius of Halifax. Overseas players were getting as much as £40,000, though some of the others just beer tokens and maybe a few extras. "I was happy enough with my £300 a game." Kevin McCallion expressed his belief in the *Courier* that teaming Jamie with Dougie Sanft and centre Craig Emmerson would give the best midfield trio in the division.

Huddersfield still had two Super League games to play when the union season commenced at home to Dudley Kingswinford on 13 September, but Tony Smith was down to his last 18 fit players and could not agree to the Ovenden Park club's bold request to release him. Jamie did sign for the rest of the season though, and ended up making 30 appearances, scoring 13 tries and two drop-goals, enough to earn the award of a First XV tie. It was a great season, with only one defeat, but that one defeat was enough to deprive them of the automatic promotion place for finishing as champions. A play-off was required against the runners-up from National Three South, Launceston, on 15 May. Though it was played at Ovenden Park, where Halifax had become virtually unbeatable, they produced their worst performance of the season and lost.

"David Brook always blamed me for the defeat," says Jamie. Halifax had fought back to score a try through prop Adam Blades in the 80th minute, but Dougie Sanft had missed what would have been an equalising conversion 15 metres in from touch. In six minutes of injury time, however, they engineered a drop-goal opportunity. "Sanft's effort was charged down and the ball rebounded to me. I knocked on and we missed our chance."

The team had also reached the Yorkshire Cup Final, a competition of which the current Halifax rugby league club were the first ever winners in the days before they switched to league. It was played the following midweek at Harrogate against an Otley side that included former Sheffield Eagles star Was Sovatabua and former Leeds winger Leroy Rivett. As if as a punishment for his knock-on, Jamie found himself on the replacements bench, but played the last 25 minutes as Halifax won through 23–21 to win the Cup for the first time since 1977.

He also won a place in the Yorkshire County team, from the bench against eventual champions Devon at Doncaster RUFC. "We didn't have a very good team, some of the big name players pulled out." It did, though, complete an interesting trio of rugby union representative appearances – Western Province, Cheshire and Yorkshire.

Now that he was almost 33 years old, rugby union might have seemed the way to play out his career – until Halifax RLFC came calling once more.

Surely this time it would not end in acrimony. Or would it?

13. Part-time at Halifax

Jamie had always got on well with the Halifax supporters, a part of the attraction of the place. Within a few months some of the keenest would be hurling abuse at him, but there was no inkling of that as the 2003–04 campaign with Halifax rugby union club came to an end with the Yorkshire Cup Final in May. By then the new summer rugby league season was well underway, Jamie having surprisingly found himself back for a third stint at The Shay.

When he had left Huddersfield he had been given a golden-handshake of two months' extra wages, around £6,000, as long as he did not join another Super League club. The money was a great help in establishing his landscaping business. There were offers from Wakefield and Salford again, which would have jeopardised the golden-handshake, plus Hull Kingston Rovers, Keighley and Doncaster in the lower leagues, but a more inviting one to return to Halifax. The manner of his departure in 2002 might have made that seem improbable, but nothing of the sort. "I was going to retire, but when Halifax rang I said yes, let's do it."

Halifax was where he lived, and suited Louise too. "It was always worrying when he was coming to the end of a contract," she says. "You worry about what's going to happen. We decided that whatever did happen, we'd just stay here and if necessary he'd travel, as with Huddersfield. It allowed us to put roots down for such as schools." In that sense, and many others, Halifax was the ideal club.

In his absence the team had been relegated from Super League in 2003, so were no longer operating with full-time players. The crippling money problems which had caused both that relegation and his own departure had been more or less resolved through the second administration, by enabling the club to finally pay off its creditors at 60p in the pound. Tribunals with Steve Linnane, Brett Goldspink and others had been settled one-by-one. On the field, the club could now look to bounce back from what was then known as National League One. The part-time contract offer to Jamie was much lower than Wakefield and Salford proposed, but fitted in well with his business activities. "The pay was very much incentive based from 2004. We would get a smallish retainer, then maybe £100 if we played, and another £250 to win."

Halifax – the club and the town – was where he wanted to be. "I have always lived in smallish places, where you can walk in the street and people will say hello. Castleford and Widnes were the same. My spiritual home in England is Wheldale, the first place I settled, where I was made welcome and never allowed to sit and mope about. But my real home is Halifax. Wakefield, away from the playing environment at the ground, would have been too big and impersonal for me, and I didn't fancy going to Salford. It was good to be still wanted by them, but also good to be able to say no."

Tony Anderson was still coach, having received no significant blame for the humiliations of 2003. "I'm delighted to have secured Jamie's services again," he told the *Courier*. "I fought tooth and nail to keep him when I arrived at the club and it was only because of circumstances at the time that we let him go."

For Jamie it would mean two games each weekend during the period of the overlap in seasons from 1 February. It was a taxing schedule, but as in the past, something to relish rather than allow to become an impediment.

Anderson was fully aware of Jamie's agreement with Halifax rugby union, and that they would have first refusal on his services until their season ended. "We have a great relationship with the union set-up," he said, "and it's something I hope to develop further." Winger Oliver Marns had returned from there too for the 2004 season, training was held there sometimes, and reserve team matches played there. "Up at Ovenden Park there were several other players who would have been ideal candidates for rugby league," says Jamie. Nothing further was to materialise though. Following the death of David Brook in 2006, the club chose to abandon professionalism, and now operate at a lower level in the rugby union pyramid.

Halifax RLFC officials were content with his union involvement as well; "I didn't do the pre-season stuff at The Shay, so they didn't have to pay me until the matches started."

Halifax expected to do well in their new surroundings. The bookies agreed, making them second favourites for promotion behind Leigh. A host of new arrivals at the same time as Jamie, among them Danny Arnold, Jonathan Roper, Alan Hadcroft, Mark Moxon, Anthony Farrell, Phil Cantillon and Chris Morley, plus Australian Pat Weisner from Leigh, gave hope of a good season.

But National League One was – and is still under its current title The Championship – a more competitive and demanding league than newcomers to it often expect. While previous relegated clubs Huddersfield and Salford had been able to retain full-time professionals, newly-imposed £300,000 salary cap regulations made that difficult, and Halifax were not entering from the most solid of foundations. Jamie had plenty of experience of it, having twice helped teams to promotion. "We have to be realistic about the prospects for the new season," he said in an interview with *Halifax Evening Courier* reporter Nick Wood. Everyone is expecting us to do well and get promoted, but we might need to consolidate and just make sure we don't get in debt again. The contracts the players are getting now are small and we are doing it because we want to help the club."

Even consolidation proved difficult. Halifax were involved for the first time in the Arriva Trains Cup, a competition that had begun in 2002 for National League sides, known first as the Buddies Cup and later as the Northern Rail Cup. Although they managed to win their group, they had been beaten 26–8 at Keighley and had lost twice to Leigh in cross-group fixtures. Meantime, Limoux knocked them out of the Challenge Cup in France, then the first three league matches, at home to Doncaster and Oldham, and away to Hull Kingston Rovers, were all lost.

Despite his rugby union commitments, Jamie had been appointed skipper. "Johnny Lawless was captain, with me vice-captain, but Johnny left and I took it on. It was another proud moment." After the defeat against Doncaster, however, he stood down. He had missed the previous game at Leigh with a groin strain, and had been a doubt for this match too, but took his place. The match proved something of a disaster. James Roberts in the *Courier* wrote that "even by the demoralising standards of last season, this was utterly abject." Jamie had actually given his team the lead with a 30-metre penalty, before "the wheels well and truly fell off" wrote Roberts, coach Tony Anderson accepting that the team's discipline was non-existent. The *Courier* encouraged text views of supporters (and non-supporters) at the time, responses including "no enthusiasm, no spark, no leadership" and "Not going again; rubbish," plus the usual calls for the coach to be sacked. Officially Jamie announced that he had a lot on his plate and felt the captaincy was affecting his form, but there was more to it than poor form or a few comments in the press.

When the team are not playing well, supporters often search for reasons. Either the coaching is at fault, or something is wrong behind the scenes, or the players are not trying. A group of them must have thought Jamie was not giving his best, or maybe it was just that he was on their doorstep when many of the other players lived away. He had been at Dudwell Lane near the Halifax General Hospital since 2002. In any case, they took it out on him, threw eggs at his front door, and a stone hit Jordan's window. "I know who they were," he says, though not with any menace. "People were driving past and calling me names, hurling abuse. These were the same people who earlier had been greeting me in the street and chanting my name in matches. For a short time I started to think of Halifax supporters in a different light, until I saw that it was just a small minority, and it was their passion for the game that was clouding their judgment."

However, the ill-feeling spread from the terraces to the boardroom. Some of the keenest supporters of all were the club's directors, in this case the former advisory group who had now taken over. One of them, Mick Stansfield, became irritated by Jamie not being at his best, particularly in the kicking department, and privately voiced his suspicions to the coach and others that Jamie must be playing badly on purpose, in order to get a pay-off from his contract. Either that, or he was betting on Halifax to lose, or win by a certain amount of points, and basing when to kick for goal on this. The comments, made in confidence, unfortunately did not remain private for long, soon becoming a topic of gossip in the bars.

To Jamie they were outrageous suggestions. He had always prided himself on the effort he gave in all matches. He was not averse to betting as was common knowledge, but that was on horses. "I was furious, and hurt by it. I can honestly say I never went out even thinking we would lose." He threatened legal action against Mick Stansfield and the club, which was averted only when Michael Steele arranged a meeting between the pair to settle their differences. A small payment from the club helped calm Jamie's anger.

Not that everything became plain sailing. There had for a while been rumours of Brad Davis, then playing in France, coming in as player-coach – he did eventually sign a playing contract, but changed his mind and joined Castleford – but Tony Anderson was replaced anyway, by Anthony Farrell. Prop forward Farrell had proved himself to be committed, enthusiastic and unremitting on the field, and it was hoped this could be spread to the rest of the team and that he could lead from the front. Unfortunately results hardly changed, Halifax remaining in the lower reaches of a division they had hoped to challenge to win. It was not too long before some of the fans were calling for Farrell to be ousted too.

"Faz is one of the most likeable people," says Jamie, "but in my opinion not best suited to management or coaching. He is too laid back. He was a tough competitor as a player, but as a coach too many people were telling him how to do things, and he listened."

Yet Jamie enjoyed being part of his regime, appreciating the understanding he showed of his day job, and the effect it had on training. Players Pat Weisner, Wayne Corcoran and Jason Boults worked for him on occasions on what could be physically demanding jobs such as building patios and driveways. "You didn't need to be doing hours in the gym after a day's work. I'd tried to explain that to Steve Linnane when I'd first got involved in it, but he was unsympathetic. He suggested if I couldn't handle it, maybe I should retire from playing. It's one of the reasons I fell out with Steve."

The arrival of Ben Black, who scored 10 tries in the last eight fixtures, helped bring a few wins, one an astonishing home victory over league leaders Leigh in August. Halifax won by 58–30 – it had been 58–12 at one point – with Jamie well to the fore. "A flawless goalkicking performance, including a couple of tricky ones from the sideline, was complemented by a great effort in general play," praised James Roberts in the *Courier*. "Bloem worked hard, tackled hard, and went forward with the ball. Farrell could hardly have asked for more." But Halifax finally finished next-to-bottom only above Keighley. It meant they had to take part in a play-off with the teams challenging for promotion from National League Two. Only the tournament winners would have a place in National League One in 2005.

Richard Agar's York City Knights, who had knocked Halifax out of the Arriva Trains Cup at The Shay earlier in the season, visited on 26 September in the preliminary semi-final. Jamie contributed four goals to a 37–20 success, but got himself put on report by referee Richard

Silverwood when he stood on the ankle of York's Australian forward Simon Friend.

He had managed to avoid visits to Red Hall for six years, but found himself charged with "conduct contrary to the spirit of the game" and facing suspension from the final. "I thought I'd be okay," said Jamie at the time, "but then again I thought I would be okay when I was accused of biting Lee Briers." A setback was a letter from York that claimed Friend had suffered serious injury as a result of being "walked on" by him, and he was found guilty. The punishment was the key. He was fined £175, but not suspended. It possibly helped that also on a charge was York winger Austin Buchanan, who was also cleared for the final after being found guilty of a high challenge on Ben Black. "We got a fair hearing," said Jamie. "There was nothing in it really. I stood on the guy, but there was no intent there and the panel accepted that."

York had won through to the final themselves by beating Workington in the major semi-final the week after losing at The Shay, so the pair met again at Jamie's former Widnes stomping ground on 10 October.

With 10 minutes to go Halifax were out of it, trailing 30–16, but came storming back to snatch a dramatic late win, Scott Grix scoring the winning try. "I gave him the pass," says Jamie proudly. Just as significant was his goal-kicking, James Roberts asserting in the *Courier* that "his five conversions – all bar one from difficult angles – proved crucial on the day." A few weeks later he roomed with York star Danny Brough, the man of the match, when they played together for Scotland. "He was saying he couldn't believe York had lost. Neither could I!"

The deal with Halifax had been for one year, which was now up. The egg-throwing made him think seriously of leaving it at that, but the season had ended positively. Although the money offered was still not very good, he retained his feeling for the club, and agreed to stay. He had not signed up for a close-season in union, so could give it his full attention. "We're very happy Jamie's staying with us," Anthony Farrell told the *Courier* in November. "He struggled early doors last year with having to play two games every weekend, but he was still one of our best players in the second half of the season." Jamie was gearing up to finish on a high. "Personally, I just want to get a good off-season under my belt and start playing again. This is definitely my last season though. Definitely."

Halifax team in 2005. Jamie is third left, back row.
(Courtesy *Halifax Courier*).

Although the off-season was fine, 2005 started badly for him with a broken finger in the pre-season friendly against Oldham, forcing him to miss the first few official matches. Warm-up games had often gone wrong during his career, with a sending-off or a bad injury, but he always liked to play in them. "I like friendlies, they're good for you. You need a hit-up, to get your body banged-up and the contact back in." Not that he saw them as friendlies. "All matches are the same to me. I play properly all the time, with my heart on my sleeve. I always felt I had something to prove, or a new coach's respect to earn."

The team fared much better. Ben Fisher came in, plus David Larder, Andy Spink, Anthony Blackwood, and later Damian Ball. Two old favourites – Damian Gibson and Freddie Tuilagi – also returned. There was a heart-warming victory over Castleford in the Challenge Cup, and progression through the group stages of the National League Cup as winners of Group 3. Major rivals in the group were Hull KR, beaten 34–26 at The Shay with Jamie in typically ebullient form. "A bad tempered Jamie Bloem and referee Colin Morris renewed their old feud," reported James Roberts in the *Courier*. He was sin-binned on threequarter time, but returned to kick two decisive late goals. Expectations had been raised, only for Halifax to lose 54–38 at Doncaster in the quarter-final.

The league season often saw the team in spectacular form, with Rikki Sheriffe, Ben Black, James Haley and the rest scoring a bucket load of tries, and Jamie converting many of them. It brought a fourth-place finish, and a first tilt at the National League One play-offs.

Celebrating a Scott Grix try in 2004

There was revenge over Doncaster Dragons in the first round, before a stunning victory away to Hull KR brought the prospect of his last ever game being a Grand Final. Castleford stood in the way, only just firmly enough when referee Karl Kirkpatrick ruled out Dave Larder's claim for a late try; Cas won 15–12. Jamie had finished his professional rugby league career on the ground where it had all begun 13 years ago.

"By then it was taking until Wednesday to recover from the weekend game, so I decided it was time to pack in. My body was taking too much." A few seasons in lower level rugby union were to follow, then Stainland amateur rugby league. When he retired as a professional player, his friends organised a surprise event for him. It followed his last league game at The Shay, a 46–20 victory over Oldham on 11 September, when he had left his white boots on the centre spot in the tradition of oversees players. Supposedly being taken for a meal at Casa in Brighouse, he found the place crowded with players from his past, plus Tony Smith and Eddie Hemmings. His boots came from The Shay to be part of an auction, which with other fund-raising activities on the night helped raise £7,000. The money might have been intended to set him up in retirement, but Louise knew where it might go. "I didn't need it", confirmed Jamie, so I gave it to the NSPCC, there and then on the night. I've always been supportive of that charity and give to them regularly."

100

14. International honours

"I have great pleasure in informing you that you have been selected in the South Africa World Cup squad as team captain."

So ran the opening sentence of a letter Jamie received in September 2000 from the South Africa Rugby League, signed by his old acquaintance Tony Lane, by then the Rhinos team manager. It was not exactly a surprise, as it had been talked about for a while, but fantastic to have confirmed. "There's nothing like captaining your country; it's the greatest thing in the world," he told journalists at the time.

He had missed the previous World Cup campaign in 1995, in which the Rhinos had also been included, as it was during the time of his suspension. His old Doncaster boss Tony Fisher had been made the coach for it, so it would have been good to have been involved; though being placed in a group with England, Australia and Fiji had resulted in three heavy defeats.

The 2000 tournament was to be staged in England and France, the group stages to commence on October 28th. The squad met up in South Africa for a training camp at the Farm Inn, Pretoria, over the weekend of 30 September and 1 October, followed by daily training sessions leading up to departure on 22 October. It was quite a commitment for him to be away from home for so long, first in South Africa, then in France where all their group games were scheduled. He would also be losing £3,000 in wages from Halifax, but the South African officials agreed to make them up, and pay a match fee on top. Interviewed by *Super League Week* before departure, he was in cheery mood. "I'll probably be a ball player of some kind," he told them. "Jesus, that's scary!"

He had not been back to South Africa much since coming to England, and took the opportunity to use some of his time on development work. "I spent five weeks in the black townships, coaching," he told *Sport365 radio* in 2001. "We had 500 kids out in a field, loving it. In South Africa, football is for blacks, although it is integrating better now, and rugby union is for whites. There's even a system where union clubs have to field two black players. I find that repulsive. If the players are good enough they should play, regardless of colour. I think the rugby union are still very racist."

Optimism had been given by pre-tournament news that a few Super 12 rugby union players, including international Dick Muir and Northern Bulls star Hannes Venter, would be available to provide extra depth, but it never materialised. Union players that did join the squad were of a lesser standard. Indeed the entire group was quite raw. Aside from Jamie, only Sean Rutgerson from Canberra Raiders at loose-forward, Salford's Mark Johnson in the centre, and Marist hooker Sean Skelton had significant league experience, though prop Jaco Booysen had played for Dewsbury a few times in 1995–96. South Africa had been in operation for eight years by then, but did not have a squad of regular players, even among the amateurs.

"Along with Rutgerson and Skelton, I was helping Paul Matete with the coaching. We quickly saw that some of them just weren't good enough. They brought in some extra ones during the preparation weeks, the squad kept changing, but they were no better. The union players didn't have a clue about the culture of the game, like getting back 10 metres. Their instinct was to run and pass, which they could do fine, but they couldn't get used to the structure that you need to be able to play successfully. We were trying to show them stuff on the whiteboard, and in drills on the training field, that you'd do with young schoolkids." The original plan was for Jamie to play at loose-forward, but he was to end up through necessity in the less familiar position of scrum-half. "My normal game was more running out wide, though I knew I would have to be a chief playmaker. Seven wasn't the right place for me, but there was no-one else to guide the team around."

Included in the preparation was a warm-up game against Wales at Loftus Stadium in Pretoria on 19 October. Wales had an experienced squad including Lee Briers, Iestyn Harris, Anthony Sullivan, Keiron Cunningham, Anthony Farrell and Justin Morgan, and won 40–8. The hope was that in the tournament itself they might meet lesser opposition. They were in Group 3, alongside Tonga, Papua New Guinea, and host nation France. On paper it seemed a less formidable group than it could have been, but in reality all three had top class players.

It all proved too much. The first match against Tonga at The Charlety Stadium in Paris was lost 66–18. The book *The Rugby League World Cup*[*] records that "Halifax Blue Sox star Jamie Bloem converted

[*] Published by League Publications Ltd.

consolation tries from centre Leon Barnard and winger Brian Best. But that only emphasised the South Africans' fighting spirit in an ultimately hopeless cause." It described Jamie as an "inspirational, not to mention emotional, skipper."

Tonga were just too strong. "Willie Mason rang rings round our boys out wide, and Tevita Vaikona scored a hat-trick. They were off-loading so we were having to make 12 or 13 tackles in a set instead of six. We couldn't get the ball to Rutgerson enough because the other players weren't good enough to."

The match against a Papua New Guinea outfit featuring Adrian Lam, Stanley Gene, Makali Aizue and Marcus Bai needed more pride and a return to respectability. "I was up against Lam at seven, and kept on standing on his foot at scrums; he wasn't happy." A supreme defensive effort at the Stade des Sept Deniers in Toulouse kept the Kumuls at bay until the 25th minute, and although they went on to win 16–0, the mission was accomplished. Jamie was spokesman at the after-match press conference: "To us that was almost like a victory," he said.

To complete the group stage, the Rhinos met a French side featuring Halifax team-mate Gael Tallec at Albi. France had lost 23–20 to Papua New Guinea, so it was a big disappointment when South Africa were humbled 56–6. Jamie was sent off early on for a perceived comment, and took the opportunity at the press conference to round on Australian referee Steve Clark. "Our boys played their hearts out, but they were playing against 14 men at all times," he was reported as saying. "He just seemed to see blue-and-white, not black-and-red. You can't go on the field and play against 14 men – it's just impossible."

The authorities reacted to the comments, disliking public criticism of referees. "I have been asked to investigate Jamie's alleged remarks," announced World Cup lead officer Greg McCallum. But he later cleared him, as he also did for the sending off. "After reviewing the available evidence I am of the opinion that the comments were taken out of context. There will be no need to take further action against the player."

By 2000 he was a veteran in terms of internationals. His appearances in the two test matches against Russia in 1992 during his amateur days had given him a thirst for more, undiminished by his move to England. Soon after his transfer to Oldham, he flew out to Russia, where the South Africans had arranged a reciprocal mini-tour. A couple of matches against club sides were followed by an international, all of which were lost, though the score in the international was close again. "It was extremely cold, and the ground was rock hard. As a referee now, I wouldn't have played them, but the Russians didn't see anything wrong."

No sooner had he got back from there, than he was off to the somewhat warmer climes of Sydney. South Africa had been invited to compete in the World 7s, a pre-season Australian tournament that had expanded to include national teams in addition to the home club sides. "We were never going to win anything as we had a lot of naive players, but it was good fun and we had a good time. Dick Muir was with us this time, but was injured in training and didn't play. Our best was Jacob Steemag, who was only small but ran like a whippet. I'm not sure rugby league 7s works. They have 9s now, which is better, though I never got the chance to play for South Africa in them."

Twelve months later, having moved on to Doncaster, he was invited to lead his country for the first time in the following season's competition, but had to pull out when his new club were reluctant to lose him. These were the days before the English and Australian seasons were aligned. "It would have been a great honour for me and it is important that South Africa as a nation do well in the competition," he told the *Doncaster Star*. "But Doncaster have some important cup and league matches coming up during the period of the tournament and after talking it over with the club officials I have decided to stay over here." A sweetener from Doncaster helped ease his regrets.

Then came his suspension, and whispers from South Africa that he would never be selected again, but that changed when he returned to action in 1997.

League Express reported as early as 17 February that "South Africa is offering an international olive-branch to Widnes full-back Jamie Bloem." SARL chairman Barry Haslam said it had not been good publicity for them when he was banned, but that now he could play a major role in establishing the game in South Africa. "We want Jamie to play a part in the future success of our international rugby league team. We need to use his experience on the field to help bring on our players." He was selected for a short tour to France scheduled for the end of the English season.

World Cup 2000: Jamie breaks through for South Africa
against Papua New Guinea.

The South African squad was mostly from the domestic competition, but had Batley's former South Sydney Rabbitohs hooker Sean Skelton as captain in addition to Jamie from England. Matches were played against Selection Girondin at Bordeaux, Languedoc-Rousillon at Carcassone, and an international against France – coached by John Kear – at Arles on 6 December. The matches were lost; 8–4, 32–24 and 30–17 in the international, but Jamie kicked six goals and won the Player-of-the-Tour award. The award had to be presented by Maurice Lindsay. "So glad to see you back where you belong," he said to Jamie, which did not go down well in view of his earlier pronouncements at the time of the ban. "I didn't reply," says Jamie. "To me he's a two-faced person. But it was a sweet moment."

In all he won 24 caps for South Africa, though some of them were unofficial matches or the 7s appearances, for which the Rhinos award caps. All of them were lost. He had slightly more luck playing for Scotland, for whom he qualified through his mother.

The 2000 World Cup had turned sour on him. The £3,000 he had been promised in lost wages was never paid, nor the fee of £400 for each match. The £150 a week allowance became £100, and he did receive that, but nothing else. The SARL did not have the money. "They should have been up front about it and not made the promises. I heard that Rutgerson and Skelton got some settlement later, but I never did. It left us a bit short. Louise and Jordan flew out for the matches in France, and we paid for that. I decided not to play for them again."

The SARL themselves had expected a higher financial return from the World Cup than they actually got, and went into something of a decline. Their fixtures dried up, but he was invited to play and help with the coaching in a series of matches against BARLA, the British amateur selection who had won the Emerging Nations tournament held alongside the World Cup. "I wasn't keen because they owed me money; I'd had by fingers burnt." He turned them down and said he wanted to play for Scotland. The Rhinos officials disapproved, so he held off until 2004, when he finally made himself available. Having been on the verge of the Scottish rugby union team while playing for Halifax RUFC, he was picked for the league side for that year's European Nations Championship.

Scotland were in Group 1 with Ireland and Wales. They got off to a winning start with a 30–22 victory in Glasgow, Danny Brough kicking five goals from as many attempts to deny Jamie the chance to take on the role himself. The Scots then looked set for the group leadership and a Final against Group 2 winners England when they led Ireland 10–3 at half-time in Navant, but fell away to lose 33–10.

Representing Scotland turned into a pleasurable experience. In charge of the team was Steve McCormack, who Jamie knew as a good, young coach, and the organisation was done well. "In Glasgow, we came out on to the field with smoke billowing and a piper in front of us playing *Flower of Scotland*. I'd never got emotional about the South African national anthem – it goes on for about six minutes – but this made the hairs on the back of my neck stand up." Unfortunately, by the time Scotland were again in action, in October 2005, Jamie had retired.

Later, in October 2008, he was asked if he would like to be South Africa's coach. "They came over here to play against amateur sides Lancashire, Cumbria, Yorkshire and the Community Lions. I was invited as a guest to the match at Leigh, where I was touted to come back, but there was still a bad taste and I chose not to."

15. Life in South Africa

If Jamie's life in rugby has been full of incident, it is merely a continuation of his action-packed years growing up in South Africa. Dodging bullets, getting suspended from school, battling pit-bulls and losing his father, certainly helped make him ready for anything rugby league could throw at him. "I was brought up hard, lots of running about. It makes you tougher. Children now are molly-coddled too much."

Despite his eventual fall out with the SARL, he had been proud to represent his country. He has always considered himself to be South African, even though he was actually born in Australia. His mother Jeannie had originated from Edinburgh, Scotland, but had been adopted soon after birth by the Johnstones, who moved to South Africa. There, after being re-adopted by the Dutch South African Huiskamp family, she was later to meet and subsequently marry his father, Eddie, also of Dutch descent. The name Bloem is of Dutch origin, meaning flowers, or keeper of tulips. Originally pronounced Blum, the English version Bloom took over. They fostered three children – Charles, Joseph and Catherine – and had a daughter of their own, Megan.

Their honeymoon had to be delayed because of his dad's work as a helicopter pilot in the South African Air Force, but early in 1971 he was granted extended leave so that the family could visit Australia, where his mum's step-parents then lived. "We decided we should see things before we had a whole gang of kids," remembers his mum, "though I was seven months pregnant when we set off." It was while aboard ship that Jamie was born, in Melbourne harbour, and he was not alone. Unexpectedly there was a twin sister, the pair being quickly transferred to Colton Women's Memorial Hospital in Melbourne itself. "They were big babies," adds Jeannie. "Jamie was 9lbs 2oz, and his twin was 7lbs 2oz." However, his sister did not make it through; Jamie was the one in intensive care, but his sister sadly died after just six days.

It was a tragic start to life in Australia, where they were to stay for three and a half years. The step-family had a farm and haulage business just outside Melbourne, where they lived until his dad was called back to the Air Force. The Angolan Civil War had started back home, and he was required for service. "I don't remember much about

Australia," says Jamie. His mum remembers it though. "He was an extremely difficult child, and baby. He was hyperactive. He would sleep for one hour in 24, and at no specific time. I couldn't go out to work because no-one would baby sit. The consultant we spoke to said it might have been something to do with being a surviving twin."

He started school in Australia, so when the family returned to Langebaan, on the West Coast 120 kilometres north of Cape Town, he joined Grade 1 at primary school, younger than the others in his class. "I was small as well. I didn't start growing until I was 16. The rest of my family were small, mum, my brother and sisters. Dad was small too, though stocky and strong. My grandfather on my dad's side was 6 feet 5 inches, which must be where my size eventually came from."

Teachers found him clever, but often hard to control. "One teacher, who was new, came round to see me," says Jeannie. "She wanted to know what I was going to do about him disrupting the class. I told her she would have to find her own way to make it work. We've become friends, and she says Jamie almost caused her to give up teaching." The way she found was to send him for a run round the school – a fairly big school – to use up his energy. Then twice round the school. "That got him into sport, and he loved it."

School started at 7.15am and finished at 1.30pm, so the shorts would be on and it was out into the fields with the gang. "There were four of us," recalls Jamie. "We weren't naughty, but a bit mischievous, and ended up doing some stupid things. There was a storm drain and we built a den in it. We brought furniture down, that we'd got from the dump or dad's hangar, an old tank battery gave us lights, and we blocked any holes to stop the wind blowing through. We charged other kids five rand to join, then, to show their commitment, they had to have a staple put in their thumb. But when the monsoons came, because we'd blocked the grates going to the river, much of the town got flooded. Our stuff got found, dad got called in and I got my backside whacked." There was another whacking when he found out about the kids with the infected thumbs.

"One of the programmes I watched on television was Batman. I'd seen Penguin jump off a building with an umbrella, which parachuted him to the ground. I tried it, jumping off somewhere, and of course it didn't work and I broke my collarbone. "I got a good hiding off dad for that later too."

108

The family was by now quite extensive. Twin sisters Laurie and Llana arrived when he was seven, to join brother Drue, five years younger than Jamie. With Megan, Charles, Joseph and Catherine, there were eight youngsters. Their first language was English, but they attended Afrikaans schools. "There was no English in primary school; nowadays when I communicate with friends from that time on Facebook, I write in Afrikaans, which I see equally as my first language. But we spoke English at home."

At school, performances in examinations determined progression through the grades as much as age. By the time he was aged 12 Jamie was struggling at maths and his dad decided that he should be held back a year. It helped, as his classmates became the same age. "Dad was a maths whiz, and wanted me to be too. Even in rugby he talked about angles of running. He hadn't played rugby himself, but did play hockey for the defence force and was good at squash and badminton. His job didn't leave much time for sport. But he did spend a lot of time with me, taking me away at weekends for my karate and tennis and athletics."

His dad got him involved in training with the Air Force guys, developing his talents. "Jamie became very good at long distance running and sprinting," says his mum. "We would have liked him to stay with the running, but he could take on any sport, though he could be a bit lazy. He'd have been okay whatever sport he chose, but his love was always rugby. We thought athletics was more his forte, but he could get rid of his aggression in rugby – it was the outlet he needed."

Because of his dad's role in the Air Force, the family moved around quite a bit. "We never had a base for long," says Jamie. "We moved from Langebaan to Northern Transvaal, then to South West Africa." Dad would still have to leave home for long periods, so we decided to move to his air base." Thus, by his early teens, Jamie was living at the base at Ondangwa in what is now northern Namibia, five miles from the border with Angola, known as the "red zone". School was at Oshakati, 30 miles away, reached on bombproof buses guarded by tanks in front and behind, and a helicopter above. The school itself was safe, but on the journey they were liable to come under attack. "It happened seven or eight times. The bullets couldn't get through the armour-plated bus windows, but it was scary being shot at."

109

Mortars fell most nights; it was often necessary to vacate to the bunkers between the houses. "You got complacent after a while in the bomb shelters, as nothing ever landed too close." During the day, being at the air base full time, we would usually eat at the Mess. There were no shops as such. The base supplied us with perishable stuff, and once a month the womenfolk went off on a bus to Tsumeb, the nearest big town, for other shopping. It was an odd way of life, a bit like camping." The houses themselves were pre-fabs, though when his dad was promoted they were able to move into a bungalow in the base.

Despite all that, life was enjoyable. "It was simple and basic, but loads of fun." There was a golf course on the base – it had no grass, but he learned to play the game there. With new mates now, it was time to build a den again. "We'd collect unexploded mortars and mines near the runways, use these and other finds to decorate the den, and use ammunition boxes to sit on. We'd eat from survival packs that we'd found or stolen. When our dads eventually discovered the den we were in big trouble; the bomb squad came in, discovered how dangerous it all was, and blew it up."

When the time came for High School, it was off to Merensky in Northern Transvaal (now Limpopo) – a boarding school, as is often the case in South Africa, with its vast size and travel requirements. Reminiscent of the old English public schools, it had a system where the new kids had to work for the seniors – and a ceremony where they made the juniors dive off a board into a compost pit. "Merensky was famous for the pit; I remember the muck being hot underneath when I did my belly flop." It was very much an agricultural school, largely self-sufficient through what it could produce. But after a while his dad felt he would be better off in a different area and sorted out for him to live with his aunt and her four kids a five hour flight away at Benoni near Johannesburg, attending Willowmoore High School, where the teaching was in English for the first time.

For the summer holidays in 1986 he went back to stay with his dad at the Air Force base in Ondangwa. "I idolised my dad, like most kids do. He used to take me up in the helicopter with him sometimes, which was great. The night of 16 July I was due to go with him again, but he changed his mind and sent me back to the hangar to listen on the radio." Jamie could tell there was trouble, but did not realise until later that the helicopter had been shot down. His father was the gunner, and the only one who died when the gun fell on him and crushed him. The enquiry revealed that despite his injuries, he had managed to crawl free for a moment and pull out his mates, who survived. He was buried in Durban, with full military honours, and awarded a posthumous medal of bravery, which Jamie was proud to receive on his behalf. "It's more than 25 years now since dad died, but it feels like just the other day to me."

"It wasn't a good time," concedes Jamie. He was still just a youngster and gave up on sport. The family had to move out of the air base, Jamie returning to live with his aunt for a while, but then deciding he would be happier back at boarding school. His mum sorted it for him, but they were no longer on the best of terms. "She bottled up her grieving, and I sort of blamed her for dad dying. I said some horrible things to her, which I greatly regret. She moved near where my aunt lived, but later left with my brother and sisters and came across to England to live, while I stayed behind. We didn't even speak for years. Everything's great between us now, but it wasn't then. Nowadays I'm a close family man, but then I was individualistic"

His mum sees it the same way. "He has never got over his dad," she says. "He listened to his dad, he was a massive part of his life, a big influence. He took it bad, personally, and went off the rails with himself. His dad was hard on him, could discipline him. With me we would end up with a row. When Eddie died, I sat Jamie down and said he'd have to be either with me or against me. He wanted to go back to boarding school. Education wasn't free in South Africa, and we couldn't really afford it, but it was where he'd be happy. We also started saving up to come over here, which took four years. Jamie wouldn't come with us. I bought him a ticket, but he wouldn't come. By then he'd met a girl in Cape Town. Jamie was born Jamie and that's how you love him. We love each other dearly, I'm proud of him, but he's a lot like me and we can't be together for long."

Back at Merensky for his final year of schooling, Jamie roomed with Jason Hartman, an English guy. "A lot of the others were religious and didn't want to share with us, so there were just two in a room for eight. We had Iron Maiden posters on the wall." Money making ventures were to the fore again. "We sawed through iron bars to make an escape route, and let kids out for money. Then we made a tuck shop in our room. A farmer about a mile away had a fruit stall, which

111

we'd raid and hide the stuff in our spare cupboards, ready to sell in the tuck shop. Years later, when I went back to South Africa to prepare for the World Cup, I went to find the farmer and say sorry. He said he never knew how we did it, so I showed him how we got in."

He was in trouble again when sneaking out to a concert – not just a few miles away, but at Bulawayo in Zimbabwe. "It was an Aids awareness concert featuring Bruce Springsteen, Tina Turner, Depeche Mode and a young Tracy Chapman. Four of us got people to cover for us and sneaked out of school in the car that mum had left behind. We parked it by the Limpopo river and swam across into Zimbabwe, where we hitch-hiked to Bulawayo and stayed in a tent. We were four white kids with no other white faces around, but the blacks took to us and treated us really well." Inevitably they failed to get away with it at school, where they were suspended for a time, given six of the best, and detentions. The sawn bars were discovered, and the tuck shop too, and Jamie and Jason found themselves returned to a big dormitory. "Luckily there wasn't much school time left. It was soon exam study time."

Jamie met girlfriend Leigh soon afterwards. "We were young, and stupid. She got pregnant, and the best thing to do was marry. I was trying to do the right thing by doing the wrong things, but I've no regrets. Tevern was born in 1992, and there was a daughter Christyn, born after we'd parted. I'd never seen Christyn, nor Tevern for 16 years, but they contacted me and I went over to Holland where they now live. They're part of the family now, they get on well with my kids Jordan and Isabelle. Mum's part of it too. We started chatting again after Jordan was born, bridges were built, and nowadays we're close again. I like this family thing now." His mum, and his brothers and sisters, went to his matches whenever they could. "He's an icon for them," says Jeannie. "He's Jamie Bloem."

National Service helped change him for the better. A somewhat daunting proposition in view of the situation in Angola, he had taken it up on leaving school, joining 101-battalion anti-aircraft. While the war did not impinge too much on the ordinary citizens of South Africa, or feature heavily on the news, it had already claimed the life of his father. "The Army taught me things about myself, and about looking out for others. I had been an angry man when dad died. I was angry with everybody, I thought everybody was against me, and I wanted to hate everybody, but it changed my outlook." The base was at Youngsville in Cape Town, near the desert, a two-day train journey away from Johannesburg, and he ended up making it on his own. The new recruits met up at a rugby stadium and spent the night sleeping out in the open air before departure. "I was bitten on the face by a spider, and got a chronic fever. Its venom attacked my nervous system. I was in hospital; it was quite serious for a time, and I couldn't travel for three weeks."

Basic training for three months meant being up at 4am, with five kilometre runs in full gear before breakfast. It was the sort of lifestyle that suited him. Inspections were less fun, with severe punishments for the whole platoon if anything was amiss. "So that our beds would be perfect, we starched the sheets and slept in sleeping bags underneath them. One of our guys knew someone in quartermasters, so we were able to get a spare set of kit which we could keep just for the inspections."

Jamie was picked for junior leadership and spent three months on that, earning his stripes as a bombardier. Given a platoon of 30, he was flown out to Lohatlha in Angola. "We were on 24 hour standby, manoeuvres in 45 degree heat, putting out bush fires caused by our shooting. It brings you together as a group of people. Based three miles away from Okokolo, where dad was killed, we spent five weeks deployed on a hill, driving pigs – land-mine proof vehicles – with a cannon on the back. We slept in foxholes, living like rats, but at the same time you could lie back and see millions of stars it was so black. The planes had gone in first to bomb the area, helicopters had cleared the area, then we anti-aircraft had to secure the high point. Ration packs arrived each week, but the water was from the tanks on the bottom of the pigs, and couldn't be wasted on showers and washing clothes. The pores on my face became pitch black."

Life there became scary. "We were rocketed and mortared at nights. Being fired at is not a fun thing to experience. They were two or three miles away, their AK–47s were inferior weapons to ours and they didn't know how to use them properly, but there was a chance that one might have been a little bit accurate. If they had known what they were doing we would have been in trouble. During the day we were on watch, but there wasn't much to watch out for. We'd fire into the trees every now and then in case anyone was sneaking up. Our cannons could fire seven or eight rounds a second, every fourth bullet with an explosive tip which would blow them up if it hit them, and every fourth one a tracer. But we never saw any action and could relax a bit after a while."

After five weeks it was a welcome return to base in Lohatlha, but news of plans for his platoon to go back to Okokolo almost immediately was too much for him. "I couldn't have handled it all over again," he admits. "Dad was important to me, so to go back for another stint where he was killed would have been difficult. I spoke to the chaplain, and we went through the base commander to negotiate an early discharge on compassionate grounds. National Service had by this time been reduced for newcomers from two years to one, which worked in my favour. I ended up doing light duties for a while until I was let out."

Compared to many, most of his army life had been quite lax, playing rugby and getting weekend passes. One weekend when there was no match he drove to his aunt's in Johannesburg, 700 miles away, on his big Honda CB900 bike, bought with some of the money left by his dad. The journey underneath Botswana was on a long straight road, a death-trap in that a driver could easily fall asleep. "It was a nice sunny Friday evening. I could see a cloud in front. It turned out to be a swarm of locusts. When they hit, they smashed my visor and I fell off. I laid there until they had passed, which must have been 15 minutes. My knees were grazed, but it was my chest that was killing me. When I looked there were red and blue marks all over it where they'd flown into me, like I'd been shot. Luckily I could still drive the bike."

National Service had been a mixed blessing. "It had been one of the best times I've ever had, but the worst time as well." Jamie was very much a daredevil in those days, so army life might have seemed ideal, but nothing of the sort. "It was the apartheid era. Some of the farm boys seemed to like the idea of fighting the little black fellas running at them through the bush. They were more interested in that than what the war was about, which none of us actually knew. But it was not for me. I was different to them and got myself out. I saw some terrible things. The koevoet, the army secret police, were sadistic. I saw captives shackled to the front of their armour-plated vehicles as they drove around, kept there until they started talking. The guys would be cut to shreds when they ploughed through the camel thorn trees. War is a waste of time if you can treat people like that. They didn't feel anything for them. Once South Africa won, they gave them the land back anyway. Dad died in that. What was it for? They could have done it diplomatically. But National Service? They should bring it back here. It would sort out a lot of these teenagers. It changed me, got rid of some of the bravado, taught me about other people and how to look after them – kids who I could hear sobbing at night. It teaches you skills, not just survival skills, but making things – ridiculous little inventions that guys came up with to pass the time."

Having left the base on his bike, he went to stay with Leigh's parents in Cape Town. The bike worried Leigh. "A teenager on 900ccs is never good. I did stupid things on it, driving between cars and scaring myself. I'd break out in a cold sweat when I'd done them."

He started working selling burglar alarms, but it only lasted a day. Seeing an advert for the SPCA – the South African equivalent of Britain's RSPCA – his love of animals encouraged him to apply for, and get, the job of an inspector. Part of the deal was a placement at the University of Cape Town, where he gained a degree in animal psychology. "It's a bit different to over here; I got a distinction degree, which means 80 to 100 per cent, but without doing much studying. I have a bit of a photographic memory that got me through. They were modular style exams that you could take when you were ready; I passed each one and just kept going."

At the same time he was working for the SPCA as a cruelty inspector, dealing with large animals, like horses, donkeys, cows and giraffes. It could be a dangerous life and they carried guns, point thirty-eight revolvers. "The people we were dealing with were a different breed, from the townships. One, who we knew as Johannes, had a 3-ton cart pulled by a horse at death's door, and carried a whip with thorns on the end of it. My usual partner was Mark Lawson, but he was off sick and a guy called Michael Daley was working with me that day, on a visit to a scrapyard in Mitchells Plain. I'd warned Johannes before for heavy loads and not shoeing his horse, so stopped him. We got a bonus for prosecutions, though I wasn't as hard as some of the others. I had a first aid box in the truck and would help people if they were trying. When he realised I was going to take his horse he got aggressive, swung an axe at me and caught me on the shoulder as I tried to duck out of the way. It was blunt and didn't go very deep, though I still have a light scar.

Working for the SPCA in South Africa.

Michael instantly had his gun-barrel to Johannes's head. I said, 'Michael, calm down, you don't have to shoot him!' and called the police."

Another time he infiltrated a dog fighting ring. "There were St Bernards, poodles and Alsatians involved, dogs you know can't really fight. I felt sick to the stomach seeing it. We got 130 convictions out of that surveillance. And death threats galore. But I was young. It didn't bother me." He worked on the arrest of a leading show-jumper, who used metal spikes and hedgehog skins on the top of fences to make his horses jump higher. "I found a surveillance post over his land; it was gratifying when we got to arrest him. He was barred from keeping animals for five years and got a 20,000 rand fine, about £1,800."

On some missions, guns had to be unclipped and escape routes planned in advance, as on a visit to a house where pit-bulls were being kept. "The farmer was wanting to fight us, and one of the dogs broke loose. I wounded it, managed to get up the wall, and was pulling Mark up when it ripped his leg. The farmer let the other dogs off and I had to shoot them all. When the farmer fell over and cried, I knew we were safe. Mark's leg needed lots of plastic surgery."

More horrific, and spooky, was an incident in a graveyard. "Benson, a black guy from the townships who worked nights, called to say there

116

were injured horses in a graveyard outside Khayelitsha. They'd either been hit by a truck, or fallen out of one. I was a senior inspector then, on stand-by, and went out. The horses were in a bad way. I called the vet and he said to put them down. Benson, a spiritualist person, was reluctant to come into the graveyard, but he had to, to hold them while I shot them. Not easy with four, as the others were spooked and bolted a bit. And it was certainly not nice. As we left, planning to return in the light, we heard hoof beats behind us. It was the last horse we had shot. It was like a horror film. Apparently muscles of dead animals can recreate the last thing they were doing. Benson turned white and dived into the thorn trees at the side. I shot the horse again and drove him home to the township, not the safest place for a white person to be. He never came back to work."

Almost as scary was his encounter with a 30 foot python. "One of Cape Town's Cape-coloureds, who were seen as second-class citizens disliked by both blacks and whites, called to say that cats and dogs were disappearing, and we drove out in the land cruiser to investigate. It was at a wooden house, built on stilts. I decided to crawl underneath, with a harness on so that I could be quickly winched out if necessary. I found an enormous python, and you could see it had eaten the dog. I catch-poled it and attached my harness so it could be winched out. We sent for back up and it took five to hold it. Our boss, Richard Burton, loved publicity and got the *Argus* to come out and cover the story, which hailed it as one of the biggest snakes found in an inhabited area. We took it to a sanctuary."

All the while, Jamie was playing rugby for Milnerton and Western Province. Taking up rugby once more in his last years at school, and continuing during National Service and beyond, had given him a focus. His ambition had once been to follow his dad into the Air Force, but it became to play international rugby for the Springboks. Star player Ray Mordt, who turned professional with Wigan, became a hero. It would have been a hard ambition to fulfil, but his switch to rugby league gave a new challenge that was reached in weeks. It meant though, that he would have to move to England.

Jamie loves his native country, and it was a great honour to represent them so many times, but he has no plans to return there. He found a new home in Halifax, is settled there now, and that is where he intends to stay.

Jamie in Scotland international colours, with Halifax team-mate Chris Birchall.

Jamie (right, back row) with Lunts Heath under-16s in Widnes.
He has coached at various levels in both codes.

16. Rugby union coach

With rugby union having figured fairly prominently throughout his league career, it was no real surprise that coaching opportunities came along in that sport. "I offered my services to Halifax RLFC, coaching the juniors, but they showed no interest," says Jamie. "Things happen for a reason. The turnover of coaches at The Shay has been high. It might have soured my affiliation with them if I'd had a bad season and been sacked."

It was Old Brodleians who contacted him first. A well-established club that was formed originally by old boys of Hipperholme Grammar School, the Brods had recently been relegated from Yorkshire 1 and were at the time near the bottom of Yorkshire 2 after a poor start to the 2005–06 season. They contacted Jamie soon after his last match for Halifax on 2 October, to offer him the position of player-coach. Although his body had told him there could be no more professional rugby league, he could manage a few more seasons as a player in union.

"I spoke to my former union coach Kevin McCallion, and he said that I should ask for £60 a session, for the Tuesday and Thursday night training sessions and the Saturday match. So £180 a week was what I suggested to Old Brods, and what I got.

"It was all about giving them belief. We stripped everything back to basics, making sure everything was done properly in matches, that we were improving our handling, passing, decision making and lines of running. We got to know each other's game, so that the runner was always confident of support. Training sessions were just basic rugby league drills, the sort of thing you would do with 10 year olds today, but it's what we needed." A Monday evening session at The Shay gym was added, for aerobic and anaerobic work on the bikes, running machines and weights. Suddenly all the matches were being won, "The place was buzzing," says Jamie. The team developed a mental toughness that enabled them to win hard or close games – and they won all 17 remaining matches to earn promotion.

Yorkshire 1 was a much tougher world in 2006–07. "The committee had said the previous year that if we won promotion, money would be made available for overseas players, and that good players who had moved on to other clubs would be persuaded to return. But it didn't happen. We went into the Yorkshire 1 season with even players from the previous year missing." Jamie himself had planned not to play, but ended up turning out in some games. "The other teams were too big and too strong for us. I tried to bring youngsters through, but we were regularly beaten and eventually relegated."

Jamie agreed a new deal for the following season with Richard Turner, the chairman, and was all for trying again. A few new players arrived and things were looking positive, but two weeks before the season everything changed. "They just came and said my services were not needed any more. I had an agreement and could have challenged it, but I decided to walk away."

A short time earlier Jamie had been a speaker at another local rugby union club, Old Rishworthians based at Copley. "I had club president Fred Dawson on one side of me and vice-captain Simon Edmundson on the other, and they talked about me going there. I was still at Brods at the time so that wasn't possible, but now it was and I rang Simon to arrange a meeting."

Rishworthians were in a much lover league, Yorkshire 5C, but offered the same money as Brods and proved to be a great club to join. They had been in Yorkshire 5 for a long time, but their years under Jamie's control were to be the most successful in their history. He asked the committee when he joined where they'd like to be in three years' time; the response was that Yorkshire 3 would be a suitable league to aim for, thus setting him his targets. "The committee provided £4,000 to spend on equipment, so we bought tackle bags, but also warm-up tops and tee shirts, which helped to make everything a lot more professional."

It was not a matter of bringing in new players. Several new ones had just arrived, including half a dozen from Rishworth School, with which the club had always been associated. Jamie had always favoured bringing young players through, and this was the line he intended to follow. He did play himself though, usually at fly-half alongside scrum-half and skipper Gary Morris, and took on the goalkicking duties. John Clough from Cleckheaton came in as a forwards coach; the pair struck up a good partnership. "We spoke on the phone almost every day," says Jamie.

"I got the team there early, both home and away. I'd have the kit already out on the pegs in the changing rooms, and we'd go out for a walk beforehand, down by the canal for home matches. Seeing us all together, dressed the same, was off-putting for the opposition when they arrived. "Bloody hell! Are we playing a professional team?" he overheard one visiting player remark. Away from home we'd sometimes arrive before the home team, so we'd park up and get together the same way."

Rishworthians lost in the opening EDF Junior Vase Cup fixture at Burley, after leading at one point 16–3, and exited the Yorkshire Silver Trophy in the first round too, but in the league matches they became unstoppable. They beat Stanley Rodillians 87–0, and eventually passed the club points in a season record of 1,004. It was the defence that proved the real strength though. In 22 league matches they conceded just 71 points, an average of 3.23, the best average in the whole of England – Market Harborough were second with 4.11.

Crucial victories were obtained over main rivals Rotherham Phoenix, then the following week over local foes Halifax Vandals in front of a large crowd. "A wonderful controlled kicking game by Jamie Bloem ensured that the home side received all spoils," ran the match report, "and the victory 17–10 was celebrated long into the night." Remaining unbeaten throughout the league season became the main focus, achieved quite comfortably in the end. Jamie himself broke the club record for points in a season, amassing 375 to easily pass the previous figure of 282. Pleasing was the progress of the young players, seven being aged 20 or less in one match against Sheffield Oaks.

For the 2008–09 season in Yorkshire 4, Jamie brought in former junior Aaron Canning, a playing colleague of his at Halifax rugby union, where Aaron had been for 17 seasons. The priority remained youth, however, the club generally fielding some of the youngest teams in its history. There were no thoughts of consolidation as they sailed through the league. Late-season defeats to Northallerton and Old Modernians left the champagne on ice for a time, but a 46–5 thumping of Leeds Corinthians sealed them a second consecutive championship – the first time in the club's history. The final match at Hornsea, won 78–0, included a night at Scarborough with the players dressed as Vikings.

The most successful period ever at Rishworthians was not about to end. They were top of Yorkshire 3 at Christmas of 2009–10, though a few later defeats saw them overtaken. "I asked the committee if they wanted yet another promotion," admits Jamie. "We were still a young team, I would not be able to play myself much longer, and Yorkshire 2 might have been too much for us. We could easily have thrown in yet more of the juniors, just missed out, and stayed in Yorkshire 3. But they preferred us to keep winning." The season ended with a victory over champions Roundhegians, ensuring they could not be caught for the second promotion place by nearest challengers Bramley Phoenix.

Although not champions, they did earn silverware when they triumphed in the Yorkshire Silver Trophy, beating Leeds Corinthians in the Final 25–22 at Pontefract. A squad consisting of 10 former junior players won through in a nail-biting finish, an Aaron Canning penalty goal in injury time seeing them home.

Jamie had already made the decision that he would not be playing in 2010. Another opening had by then come along for him as a rugby league referee, increasing commitments in that field meaning that he would not even be able to attend most of the matches on a Saturday afternoon. "I wanted to stay on as coach, and did so. They wanted me to play though, and in November said they'd rather I wasn't there if I couldn't get to the games." The team were inevitably having a tough time in Yorkshire 2 and losing regularly. John Clough took over, along with Michael Piper who had joined earlier from Castleford. "I'd let them take on more and more while I was there – maybe that was a mistake," says Jamie. "I enjoyed it there, and would go back."

Soon afterwards he was contacted by Gary Ellis, who asked if he knew anyone who might be interested in coaching Stainland Stags Amateur Rugby League Club in the lower reaches of the Pennine League. Jamie was happy to lend a hand himself. Refereeing commitments were now more in the summer months, while Stainland still played in the winter, so he was able to play quite regularly as well as coach. In a press feature in 2012, Ellis was quick to give him praise. "Jamie is doing a fantastic job," he said. "Last season we won eight of his nine games to clinch promotion to Division 4. He's instilled discipline. Pre-Jamie we forked out £1,400 in fines, but we have not been near the disciplinary board this season."

Not that controversy was over. A report in *The Sun* newspaper in February 2012 claimed that he had been sent off against Silsden Park Rangers for referee abuse. He hadn't played in the match, and there was later a retraction.

He also turns out in two-handed touch games for Great Britain Legends, "even though I'm not one", when he can. "Barrie McDermott plays, and Steve Hampson, Ikram Butt, Martin Dermott, Neil Cowie, Andy Gregory, Gary Schofield, Darren Rogers, Gary Connolly. Colin Morris usually referees. It gets us old players together, and raises money for the Life For A Kid charity."

He even played again for Halifax at The Shay against Burleigh Bears in James Haley's testimonial match in October 2011 at the age of 40. "I enjoyed it immensely, and it made me think I'd packed in my rugby league career too soon. There had been opportunities to join Wakefield Trinity, and more recently Jason Demetriou had talked about lending some experience to Keighley in Championship 1. Remembering how long it had started to take to get over games, I had quickly turned them down, but now I wonder."

A renewed involvement in professional rugby league had long appealed. Before the refereeing took hold, coaching was always in his mind. In late 2008 a job became available at Oldham, as assistant to Steve Deakin. "Deaks had been an assistant coach himself at Huddersfield when I was there. I had a Level 2, and half a level 3, coaching certificate at the time, so I contacted him. He arranged an appointment with chairman Chris Hamilton, who seemed to like what I had to say, and a second interview was fixed at which I was asked to take session plans for weights, conditioning, diets etc. I spent two and a half weeks planning them. Deaks went for me, but the club appointed Mark Cass instead because of his greater experience."

It was that decision that confirmed his preference to go into refereeing, which he had recently started. "It made my mind up for me, so it turned out for the best in the long run."

He was later offered a coaching job at Halifax rugby union club, now in the lower leagues following financial difficulties and a move to amateur players only. However, he opted to remain with Stainland, where a second consecutive promotion was achieved in 2011-12, before bowing out of coaching at the end of the season.

Celebrating success with Halifax.

17. Poacher turned gamekeeper

"The referee was having a shocker. I was commentating for Radio Leeds at a Friday night game between Leeds and St Helens in 2008, and said so. On Monday I got a phone call from referees' controller Stuart Cummings, who said he had been listening, and didn't want me saying things like this about referees. I've never been one to hold back, and always said what I think. I must have said that referees made errors because they hadn't played the game, and that I could do a better job myself, because eventually in the phone call he asked me if I fancied doing it."

It was something that appealed to Jamie. He had had his share of problems with referees over the years, including questioning them and challenging them, but he felt it was something he could do. "Not many could. But I'm thick-skinned and don't mind the abuse. I'd faced plenty before."

He met up with Stuart Cummings at the Cedar Court hotel at Ainley Top, where he was told that former players were a priority for the Rugby Football League. Many referees were failed players or young kids, so experience of playing in professional rugby league was lacking. A fast-tracking system was available to the right candidate.

So Jamie did the referees' course and exams. "People thought it was a joke because of my past, but I was going to stick it out." The course showed him that despite some 15 years as a player, he did not even know all the rules, but he completed it successfully and was quickly thrown in at the deep end. The fast-tracking meant that his first match was Oldham reserves against Rochdale Hornets reserves, which was daunting. "I wasn't ready really. I was out of my depth." He did some Conference matches, college games on Wednesday afternoons, and National Youth League under–18s, but soon afterwards broke his leg playing rugby union, and was sidelined for a period. By the time he was fit again the fast-tracking system had come to an end and he had to start all over again. "That was annoying at the time. I felt I'd been stitched up. But I was stubborn enough to stay, and it turned out to be for the best. Players had been taking advantage of my inexperience; I didn't have the man-management skills to deal with it then. Fast-tracking doesn't work for that reason."

What he did quickly realise though, was that his attitude to referees when a player had been wrong. "It was a lot harder than I had thought, because you have to make split-second decisions. I'd have behaved differently towards referees if I'd known what I do now."

He was in the Halifax Referees' Society initially, though later left to join a breakaway Calderdale group. Neither has had much luck recently in producing talent for the professional ranks. Nick Oddy, whose son Sam played in Jamie's Stainland side, made the grade a few years back, preceded by top flight officials Jim Smith, Ronnie Jackson and Henry Mason, and before them Walt Hemmings. There have been no other former Halifax players, though Wilf George, Johnnie Blair and Brendan White are among those to have impressed in the amateur game, and Halifax Hall of Fame member Cyril Stacey took charge of professional second team matches in the Yorkshire Senior Competition after retiring as a player in 1929.

The system without fast-tracking was a better one. "I was being guided through properly, gaining confidence. Just like when you're a player, you've got to learn patterns and routines. You have to learn where to be, how to move, and what to look for. It helps that I understand the calls the players are making, where they're going on the field, and can get there with them." His learning process took him to some primitive locations. "I've changed in a broom cupboard for an under–18 game in which all they wanted to do was fight."

One of the strangest venues of all was Gothenburg, where he officiated at a Sweden versus Norway international. "I was excited to get that. I was flown over for the full weekend, put up in a hotel that no-one had paid for – though that was soon sorted. I was on the 11th floor, from where the bloke on reception said there would be magnificent views, but Gothenburg has to be the ugliest city I have been to. It was all concrete, no glass buildings. And a 30-line railway track outside the hotel." An earlier inspection of the pitch had shown no lines marked out, and though he had been promised it would be done, he made sure he got there early. "It was pouring with rain, and they said it couldn't be marked. So with some of the players helping, we found some whitewash, and between us we got it measured out, then marked. It was an awful stadium, with Portacabins for changing rooms. Not what I thought my first international would be like, and as grassroots as you can get. But marking the pitch had brought us all together, I got to know the players' names – which is what the RFL encourage us to do – and the match was a good, close one. The standard was low, but some of them were ice hockey players and they put in some frightful hits. We had a right old party after."

Refereeing at the lower levels can be unappealing, and might help explain why top former players have not taken it up. That, plus the fact that there were once rules that if Grade One had not been reached by the age of 40, the limit would be as a touch judge. "Referees get a lot of stick from fans and there's a type of stigma attached to the job which makes it seem uncool. Not every player could be a referee. You have to have a strong character, be able to take immense criticism from players, supporters and the game's hierarchy." But for Jamie, progression was soon to follow.

In 2011 he was promoted to reserve grade. "Officially I was grade 3, but reffing Grade 2 games." He missed out of the under–20s Grand Final, but did get the Summer Conference Final. He also got a Sky Sports Championship game at York on the line, when the cameras followed him round. "It's an acquired taste. The more abuse I get, the more I smile. I can be quick and witty and give it back. At a Rochdale Hornets versus Oldham game an old fellow was following play along the touchline and giving me abuse. When his team scored in the corner and the conversion was being lined up, he was calling me dumb, and saying I had been as a player too. 'Listen,' I said. 'You've paid to watch me play, and you've paid to watch me ref. Who's the dumb one now?' I bought him a beer after the game. Hopefully I changed his perspective."

In professional matches of course, he knows a lot of the people involved. At Leeds, for example, Brian McDermott and Damian Gibson were involved with the under–20s, and at Warrington there was Richard Marshall. Speaking as a panel member at a Halifax Supporters' Trust meeting that Jamie chaired in March 2012, Marshall told of how he saw him at a Warrington under–20s match and wondered why he was there. "You were one of the dirtiest, horrible players," he jokingly told him. "I couldn't believe you were the referee."

In Jamie's view, it all works to his advantage. "I have a good rapport with a lot of coaches," he says. "I played with some of them, and you try to do your best. Sometimes they'll have a go. I'm open to anyone to come to me. As long as they chat to me rather than chat at me. I used to chat at referees, but you can't do it. The players as well will vent their frustrations at you sometimes because you're the nearest to them, and again, as long as it's within reason, I'm okay with it. I try to use my experience as a player. I know how they feel because I've been there. I've only sent one player off in three years because I like to keep everyone on the field. I'm not proud of the sending off, but it was for spitting at another player, which I found disgusting."

Despite his tolerance, dissent can be a problem. "A referee needs to be strong, but not cocky, and have fun with the players."

Then in 2012 came Grade 1, and the chance for the press to dub him the ultimate poacher turned gamekeeper. Other new referees were appointed at the same time, the plan being to introduce them gradually, with new teams scheduled to be added to the Championship leagues in 2013. Jamie started with Toulouse versus Keighley in the Northern Rail Cup, followed by a return to one of his former homes when he took charge of Oldham versus Dewsbury. It was 19 years after he had played for Oldham, though now the venue was Whitebank rather than Watersheddings on the other side of town. Roger Halstead was still there to see it. "I thought he had a fine game," he commented, "commanding the respect of both teams and handling it efficiently and with a minimum of fuss. The referee in this game was NOT the main topic of discussion by fans or the rival coaches after the game and I reckon that is the biggest compliment any man in the middle can receive."

In May he was able to officiate a second of his former clubs when he took charge of Doncaster's match at North Wales Crusaders, and he ran the line in a Halifax game at The Shay.

In a series of firsts, he was thus the first to complete the transition from player to referee in the Super League era, the first to both play and referee in the Northern Rail Cup, and the first to both play for and referee Oldham and Doncaster.

As a player, there had been some referees he had not got along with. "There were some I felt had it in for me, that I'd always get sin-binned with. It brought out the worst in me, I never wanted to work with them and help them out. Karl Kirkpatrick was a top class referee, and a big loss to the game when he left, but you couldn't talk to him. Steve Cross, another good referee, sin-binned me twice in one game when I was at Doncaster. I liked referees who were characters. I loved watching Bill Harrigan, the Australian, though I never played under him. He made a drama out of things and liked to be the centre of attention; I'm not looking to copy that. Ian Ollerton was another, and John Holdsworth. John was very vocal, shouting instructions, tapping you to get off the tackle. You knew where you were with him." Among more recent officials, Jamie always enjoyed playing under Ashley Klein. "He only sin-binned me once, and on that occasion, once he'd called me over and explained, he almost made me feel thankful for it."

He doesn't exactly model himself on anyone as a referee, but does try to be a bit like Holdsworth and, though he was one of the quieter ones, Klein. "I want players to think I'll give them a chance. I want them and me both to have fun. I try to get involved with them a bit, have a giggle with them sometimes. I'm vocal, loud, want them to know why a decision has been made. It helps that I've played against some of them, helps get respect."

The radio summarising runs alongside. He had never been short of an opinion, and always had plenty to say for himself; he had always been happy to give a post-match interview in either the club bar or for radio, while in his days at Doncaster he had written a weekly column, "The Rhino Reviews" for the *Doncaster Advertiser*. The radio work started when he did an hour's programme with James Deighton for BBC Radio Leeds on his career. "It must have sounded good because he suggested I try summarising. When Halifax played Huddersfield at The Shay in a friendly, Johnny Lawless was summariser, but he could only stay for the first half, so I did the second."

James Deighton himself traces the start back a little further. "In 2003 I was at the McAlpine Stadium to interview Huddersfield Giants coach Tony Smith," he recalls. "While I waited I found myself chatting to a strange bloke with an even stranger accent. I seem to remember he was wearing an odd woolly hat as well. He was telling me about growing up in South Africa and I was impressed with the way he told the story and at the time I thought it would be great to get this strange accent on the radio in some shape or form." The opportunity arose after he had rejoined Halifax. "As I would soon discover, involving all things with Jamie, he jumped at the chance to give it a go and the rest really is radio history."

The two have since become good friends. "He was a witness at our wedding in 2006 when he turned up at the hotel asking for 'foreigners' discount', which he duly got," adds Deighton. "Our families are incredibly close and I have watched his children grow up with pride and he ours."

The radio work went well. "I get some good games now," admits Jamie. "I'm honest and up front and say what I think. Apparently they get more text messages when I'm on because of what I say, which they like. I've worked with some other good commentators, like Ron Hill and Terry Crook, and I've also done a lot with Radio Five Live."

His pal agrees. "On the radio Jamie's insight, enthusiasm and humour has seen him continue as one of our leading summarisers. His presence at matches has helped in other areas too. While we were commentating on a game once a 'disturbance' broke out right in front of us. Jamie calmly finished his sentence and, as I continued live on air, he stepped in to diffuse the situation. The look on the two blokes' faces was priceless. Jamie then picked up his microphone again and carried on as if nothing had happened."

Radio work is fun for Jamie and he sees games he would not usually attend, with trips away to such as the Magic Weekend and Wembley. "I'm getting paid to go to these games and talk for two hours!"

Being paid to do something he enjoys has been a way of life. Aside from the spell plumbing when he was in Doncaster, he had been a professional rugby player since his arrival in the country until he set up his landscaping business. Things could change if he becomes a full-time referee. "I hope to get there," he told the *Courier* in 2012. "In every walk of life you look for progression." As a player he never made a Challenge Cup Final, or a Grand Final, but that did not make him a bad player. Similarly if a Super League refereeing chance never came along, that would not make him a bad referee. "If I was offered a full-time role I would take it," he says, though time might not be on his side.

Louise believes he would give it his all. "He's rugby league through and through. He was so passionate about what he did on the field, was always there early at a game, and it's the same with refereeing today. Everything's got to be 100 per cent. I just wish his dad could see him now. He pushed him through sport, and influenced all this. He'd be so proud. It's a shame he can't see it."

Appendix: Statistics and records

Rugby league

British professional clubs

		App	Sub	T	G	DG	Pts
1992–93	Castleford	0	1	1	0	0	4
	Oldham	11	1	2	0	0	8
1993-94	Doncaster	31	3	8	4	0	40
1994-95	Doncaster	10	0	9	0	0	36
1997	Widnes	20	7	14	37	3	133
1998	Widnes	12	0	9	1	0	38
	Halifax	13	8	9	5	0	46
1999	Halifax	15	0	4	8	0	32
2000	Halifax	29	0	6	27	0	78
2001	Halifax	15	8	6	44	0	112
2002	Halifax	18	10	6	21	2	68
2003	Huddersfield	18	4	3	11	0	34
2004	Halifax	26	1	9	91	1	219
2005	Halifax	11	13	1	68	0	140
Total		**229**	**56**	**87**	**317**	**6**	**988**

Internationals

South Africa

		App	Sub	T	G	DG	Pts
1992–93	Russia (h)	2	0	0	6	1	13
1992–93	Russia (a)	3	Details not available				
1993	World Sevens (Sydney)						
1997	France (a)*	3	0	0	6	0	12
2000	Wales	1	0	0	0	0	0
	World Cup	3	0	0	3	0	6
Total		**14**	**0**	**0**	**15**	**1**	**31**

* Two matches against club sides, one against France

Scotland

	App	Sub	T	G	DG	Pts
2004	2	0	0	0	0	0
Overall Total	**243**	**56**	**87**	**332**	**7**	**1,019**

British amateur rugby league
Stainland Stags (player-coach)

Rugby Union

South Africa
Milnerton
Western Province under -20
Western Province

France
Racing Club (Paris)

England
Thornensians
Widnes
Halifax
Old Brodleians (player-coach)
Old Rishworthians (player-coach – club record 375 points in 2007–08)
Cheshire (1 appearance)
Yorkshire (1 appearance)